PRA

POLITICALLY HOMELESS

'This book made me laugh out loud – and wince in recognition'
Tony Blair

'It would be impressive for anyone to bring such surgical preci-
sion to either comedy or political analysis. Forde's ability to bring
it to both – in spades – is truly remarkable. A sparkling jewel of
a book' **James O'Brien**

'The second funniest book I have read about being a Labour
supporter from Blair to Brexit' **John O'Farrell**

'This book is smarter and funnier than Donald Trump. Matt
Forde was so bad at politics that I'd have considered working for
him' **Anthony Scaramucci**

'That Matt Forde is able to make the current political shit-show
funny shows his genius. You'll be laughing too hard to notice,
but this is a very clever book' **Ruth Davidson**

'Definitely one of the books I will claim to have read this year'
Jack Dee

'Absolutely brilliant. I didn't want the book to end but I'm glad Fordy's political career did. And I mean that as both a compliment and not a compliment' **Russell Howard**

'Wise and witty – the must-read (and will-make-you-laugh-out-loud) confessions of a political obsessive. Dazzling stuff' **Gyles Brandreth**

'Anyone who has ever seen Matt Forde on stage knows he's funny, smart and politically spot on. So is this book' **Alastair Campbell**

'Passionate, hilarious, thought-provoking and packed with political insight and life wisdom' **Emily Dean**

'Matt Forde is one the cleverest and funniest people I know. He has managed to find humour and insight in a time when they are sorely missing from not only politics but life in general. This book is better than mine and I hate him for that' **Jon Richardson**

'Matt Forde is one of my favourite comedians and this book is fantastic' **Vicky McClure**

'Matt Forde is one of the funniest people I have ever met. He is also one of the most underrated political commentators in the country. Read this book if you want to learn about politics and laugh at the same time' **Rob Beckett**

'Searingly insightful and laugh-out-loud hilarious' **Peter Mandelson**

'Matt Forde's love of politics seems to have brought him only pain. Luckily his account of his own suffering is a hilarious read for the rest of us' **Josh Widdicombe**

'Matt Forde proves that the personal is political, and that it can be very funny too' **Al Murray**

'This is the funniest book I've read in ages' **Jess Phillips**

'A truly rare breed of political comedian who succeeds in being hilarious whether you agree with him or not' **James Acaster**

'Also politically homeless, I expected to either laugh or cry at this book. I cried with laughter' **Kezia Dugdale**

'Funny and approachable, just like Matt himself' **Jeremy Vine**

'Insightful, witty and measured, it's the perfect political antidote to politics right now!' **Rachel Riley**

'Laugh-out-loud funny' **Ian Rankin**

Matt Forde is a stand-up comedian and TV, radio and podcast host from Nottingham whose weight fluctuates wildly. As well as hosting four series of his own political comedy TV show '*Unspun*', Matt has also appeared on *The Royal Variety Performance, Have I Got News for You, Mock the Week, 8 Out of 10 Cats* and Channel 4's *Alternative Election Coverage*. A former Labour advisor, his hit podcast 'The Political Party' has amassed more than 6 million downloads and reached the top of the iTunes comedy chart. He has been described as 'our foremost satirical stand-up' by *The Times* and sells out his entire run at the Edinburgh Festival every year. Outside of politics and comedy, he is a fan of Nottingham Forest and curry.

POLITICALLY HOMELESS

MATT FORDE

Quercus

First published in hardback in Great Britain in 2020 by
Quercus Editions Ltd

This paperback published in 2021 by

Quercus Editions Ltd
Carmelite House
50 Victoria Embankment
London EC4Y 0DZ

An Hachette UK company

ISBN 978 1 52941 279 6
EBOOK ISBN 978 1 52941 278 9

Typeset by CC Book Production
Printed and bound in Great Britain by Clays Ltd, Elcograf S.p.A.

Papers used by Quercus are from well-managed forests and other responsible sources.

For Josie, my mum.
(Sorry about the rude bits)

CONTENTS

Introduction   1

Finding a Political Home   5
Tribalism   19
Ideology, Principles and Mindset   33
The Power of Individuals   43
Party Conferences   59
Tricks of the Trade   83
Early Warning Signs   113
UKIP FM   139
The Decline of Political Language   153
The Curse of Complacency   167
The Collapse of the Centre   183
The Rise of Political Bullying   195
The Podcast   219
Conclusions   237

Acknowledgements   245

INTRODUCTION

Hello and welcome to my first book. I'm as surprised as you are.

Whether you bought it, borrowed it or stole it, I hope you enjoy it. Although if you did nick it, please consider doing the decent thing and transferring the value of the cover price directly into my bank account.

I'm a stand-up comedian, so I only usually write material that's meant to be performed in front of a live audience. It's odd to create something where for once I won't be able to hear your raucous laughter and repeated rounds of applause. Who knows, maybe if everyone reads it at the same time, I will? I'll listen at my window. If it's quiet, I'll just presume you've given it a standing ovation.

As someone who wanted to remain in the EU and who worked for the Labour Party before it became a racist cesspit, the last few years haven't been great for me politically. It feels like everything I care about is being lost. I know that millions of other people feel this way. You may be one of them. If so, I hope this book helps provide some comfort. If not, you can use it to rest your laptop on or to throw at next door's cat when it shits in your garden.

It started around the age of nine. The politics obsession, I mean. I realise that made it sound like it was going to be a story about something else. Don't worry, I wasn't groomed or anything – it's not that sort of book. The politics obsession has never left me. I threw myself into it in the way that normal people would get into bands. Despite the absolute howling mess that everything has become recently, I'm still a hopeless obsessive.

The politics of Brexit and Corbyn were a pincer movement from right and left which drowned out reasoned debate and helped create a culture war where nuance is not tolerated. Opponents weren't human beings who thought differently, they were enemies who needed to be humiliated. I don't like this approach to life and it's this cultural change in politics that has alienated me the most.

Politics intrigues those who haven't been involved in it. They're never sure whether it's as chaotic as they might imagine. Having worked in it, I can tell you this: it's way worse than you imagined. I've included some stories from my time in politics to show you how incredibly weird things really get. Working in politics is like being trapped in an escape room with the thickest and angriest people you can find, and then being amazed that you can't get out.

Throughout the book you will find a few key lessons I have learned from my career in politics. I learned these the hard way, usually through humiliating personal failure or by witnessing someone else's humiliating personal failure. Because nobody gives you a 'how to' list, you just get on and do it. It's often only when you break one of the rules that you find out it even exists. These lessons are particularly useful if you want to become a politician, and they have been tailored accordingly.

In part this is a memoir, but it's also my perspective on how politics, particularly in the UK, has gone to hell. We didn't get here by accident. People who should have known better took decisions that led us here. As frustrated as I've become, I've tried to remain as positive as possible. There's a lot to be annoyed about so the book reflects that, but it also contains some optimism and, in lieu of that, some jokes.

So, however you've come into possession of this book, whether you have similar politics to me or whether this was the last book on the trolley at the prison library you were incarcerated in for book theft, I hope you enjoy it.

Matt Forde
London, August 2020

Chapter 1

FINDING A POLITICAL HOME

My name is Matt Forde and I'm a political obsessive. There, I've said it. I made that pretty clear in the introduction, but I want to be absolutely certain that you know what you're in for. I'm consumed by anything to do with politics and I am beyond help. I love every part of it – the ideas, the individuals, the debate, elections, committees, scandals, inquiries, budgets, mistakes, the lot. Every tedious element of it engages me. Nearly all the books I read are about politics. The first thing I do in the morning is check news sites and social media to find out what's happening in the world (lots) and to see if anyone's called me horrible names (lots). The political institutions enchant me; I love going to Parliament buildings and council chambers in the same way that I enjoy going to football stadiums for the first time. Although I conduct myself differently there, of course – I drink way more when I'm at Parliament.

What's slightly odd is that this obsession began very early on in my life. I was eight years old when Margaret Thatcher resigned, and I remember the day clearly. A punk rocker with a ghetto blaster walked past my mum, my sister and me on our way into town, and shouted, 'She's out! She's fucking out!' I guessed he wasn't talking about my mum being out of the house, as she did this most days and it wasn't news. I asked her what he meant, and she told me that the prime minister had resigned. At that age I couldn't appreciate the magnitude of the event, but I knew it was serious. The image is still so clear in my head, mainly because as the bloke walked past us, I noticed he had two massive holes in the back of his leather trousers for his backside to hang out of. Not only that, he had an eye tattooed on each bum cheek. That experience had an effect on us. It triggered my love of politics and my mum's love of flashing her tattooed bare arse at strangers.

The next thing I know, it's the 1992 election. I'm nine at this point and I'm desperate for Labour to win. Like most memories of childhood, I recall it being a bright sunny day. There were red and yellow Labour posters in everyone's windows, which made it look like the whole street was decorated with bunting. Suddenly, a car with loudhailers burst on the scene. It was covered in Labour branding and balloons, and the people inside it were handing out stickers and posters. It was like the ice cream van had turned up. The kids swarmed it, grabbing at all the goodies they could. The Conservative Party victory was a powerful early lesson that just because everyone around you is voting a particular way, it doesn't mean that the rest of the country is. Undefeated, I proudly displayed my Labour stickers in my window next to my Nottingham Forest ones. Maybe I was just into teams in red who are lost causes.

I'm not sure why I cared so much at that age, because I didn't grow up in a heavily political home. My mum was a Labour voter but wasn't a member or even an activist; we didn't know anyone in politics and there were no political books in the house. It was the opposite of Ed Miliband's upbringing – and we only had one kitchen. We didn't discuss Marx, Engels or Luxemburg.

On the other hand, we did talk a lot about ethics, values and fairness. My mum had been a nun before she'd had me. (She wasn't having it away with a priest or anything, I came along a couple of years later.) We went to church every Sunday, so I guess that was good preparation for going to Labour Party branch meetings: a load of old people in a freezing hall listening to some bearded bloke drone on about the past. I realise now most of them were only there for the red wine. To my mum's mild disappointment, I'm an atheist now, but the structure that religion gives you, plus the weekly focus on a moral discussion, probably gave me an underlying desire to be part of something that would do good in the world.

Joining the Labour Party was the obvious choice for me, although it didn't feel like a choice at all. I grew up in a single-parent family on benefits, in inner-city Nottingham, under the Thatcher and Major governments. Of course, there are plenty of working-class Tories and there always have been, but there's something about being on benefits that's different. What little Thatcher offered to some of the working class didn't benefit us. My mum couldn't afford to buy her housing association house. She was too busy being a full-time mum to two children to start a business. She had my sister Ruth and me reading and writing early, instilled in us a strong work ethic, ensured we were raised in a loving and supportive house and that we had hot, healthy dinners when we came back from school. She was basically a single mum breaking her back to give her two kids the very best start in life in a tough part of Nottingham, in poor housing and on no money.

Women like my mum should have been hailed as heroes, as the backbone of the country, sacrificing their own futures so that their children could thrive. That's not what happened. The Tory government of the day launched a vicious moral campaign against so-called 'broken homes' and specifically single mothers. Even as a kid it struck me as spectacularly dense to attack single mums because, by definition, they were the ones who'd stayed to raise the children. Shouldn't absent fathers have been the issue? It's like someone berating the few people who turn up to a house party because no one else has shown up. They're not the ones who've let you down. Luckily, as well as having a wonderful mum, I also have a wonderful dad, so I've not been let down at all. Well, I have a bit. He supports Liverpool and prefers rugby to football, so it's a good job I grew up with my mum.

What could be a more political upbringing than that? Like I said, we weren't sat around discussing lofty ideas about the role of the citizen and state in a civil society, I had no idea about the judiciary, executive and legislature, we weren't critiquing Keynes or Hayek, but we were living at the sharp end of every political decision taken by the government. A sense of injustice created my politics. I knew that we were disadvantaged, and I wanted to do something about it.

That feeling has never left me. Apart from the desperate unfairness of it, the estates full of untapped talent and potential mean we're all worse off. There are millions of people in the UK who are written off because of the fate of where they were born, because of a postcode lottery. To be clear, I'm not talking about the Postcode Lottery people on the TV advert, although I've never seen them on my street with their big shiny cheques, the bastards. If they'd have shown up and showered us with cash when I was a kid, maybe I'd have been a Tory instead.

So there I was, a Labour kid, in a general way. I didn't know anything about the history of the party, how it operated, what its structures were, what its policies were, and I was a child. I was a football fan applying that to politics – Labour were my team, the Conservatives were my opponents. I didn't know much about football back then either because, as I just mentioned, I was a child. Some people who've heard my football radio shows and podcasts would say that I still know very little about it but hey, that's the joy of social media. Being Labour was already part of who I was, but it was one amongst a number of other passions: Nottingham Forest, *ThunderCats*, *The A-Team*, football stickers and Nottingham Forest. It was only really around the time I went to secondary school that I realised my love of politics was becoming far more important.

Place shapes you, but so does time. Up until this point, all I'd ever known was a Conservative government. Just at the moment when I was really starting to develop my thinking, to read about politics, to figure myself out, Tony Blair became leader of the Labour Party.

Labour felt young, vibrant and exciting. The tone of Britain was changing; it felt like a time of hope and optimism. What seemed to emerge was that people from my sort of background could go on and achieve things. All my football heroes were working class. I adored Oasis for their music, but I also strongly identified with their class pride. Being skint meant you had to work harder, but it wasn't something to be ashamed of. Not everyone wants to be or can be a footballer or a rock 'n' roll star, and that's where Tony Blair came in. The changes he would make would allow disadvantaged children to find their way into better jobs and education in whatever field they chose in record numbers. I wanted to be a part of that.

I wrote to Tony Blair when I was fourteen, asking how to join the Labour Party. I got a very polite reply back from a correspondence secretary informing me I had to be fifteen to join. I was livid. I had to wait ONE WHOLE YEAR?! I was already in too deep, itching to get involved, and I couldn't believe they wanted me to wait so long. The secretary enclosed a signed photo of Blair, presumably to soften the blow. This gave me an idea. I'd always collected football autographs when I went to Forest games. Why stop there? I began to write to every cabinet minister asking for a signed photo. I've got all of them. Well, my mum has. There's a whole collection of gracious letters from bemused civil servants from now defunct government departments like the DfEE, DLETR and MAFF. I always had a soft spot for MAFF (Ministry for Agriculture, Fisheries and Food) as it's what my sister Ruth used to call me – because it sounded like my name, not because I ate so much I could have been minister of food.

The other thing I did was join the Socialist Workers Party. One Saturday I'd been walking through Nottingham and seen their stall. I know now that I should have kept on walking, but I was the sort of dozy fool who would stop and talk to anyone with a flyer. They were rebellious, passionate and they had trestle tables. What wasn't to like? Well, quite a lot, actually, but that came later. I got immediately involved. Before I knew it, I was going round to these people's houses, sitting on their floor and listening to them talk about Karl Marx and Rosa Luxemburg. I was taking it all in – and becoming more convinced that a revolution was imminent. At the time of writing, the revolution hasn't happened yet. If it has by the time you're reading this, feel free to burn this book to keep you warm. That also goes if there hasn't been a revolution.

Emboldened by all this intellectual ammunition, I did what every normal schoolboy does and made socialist propaganda posters to plaster over the school noticeboards. I got a light bollocking for it and deservedly so. What an idiot, wasting those sun-drenched breaktimes to pin up information about what the chief executive of Magnet was paid compared to his staff. This was in the nineties. Everyone else was outside listening to Oasis and pretending to be Gazza. I was poncing about pretending to be Arthur Scargill. To be fair, I was listening to Oasis and pretending to be Gazza too, but I was the only one trying to foment revolution.

Out of school, I rapidly rose through the ranks of my local SWP branch and was put in charge of selling a quarterly called *Marxism Today*. I was dizzy with responsibility and didn't really know what it meant. Well, what it meant was I was one of only three people to turn up to that branch meeting so I couldn't say no. There was a buzz to having a role; I was being treated like an adult and I felt valued. They never patronised me or made me feel small for not knowing things. I loved their passion – they were angry about all the right things: poverty, inequality, low pay and injustice. However, as I soon discovered, they were angry about everything. Including things that, even at fourteen, I didn't think they should be angry about.

Labour had not long been elected and after seeing how happy it had made my mum and so many other people, I thought the SWP guys would be fairly on board with it all. What a mistake. Oh no, they hated Tony Blair as much as they hated Margaret Thatcher, and this was in 1997. At that stage I had no idea about how parties worked, or their structures. At one SWP meeting I was invited to attend the Labour Party conference. This was like being offered tickets to the FA Cup Final. Of course I'd like to go, do we need a ticket? 'No, we're going to protest outside of it.' Oh well, it would still be fun to be outside and to catch a glimpse of the prime minister, the cabinet and all the other stuff that goes along with it.

I never got as far as the Labour conference, though, because before that I'd gone to the SWP conference and it scared me right off. We had taken a Transit van down from Nottingham to London. This sounds mad now but back then London felt as exotic and distant as New York. How exciting: I'm learning all about these big ideas, I'm reading all these books (which I don't really understand but that's not the point, I think I must be absorbing some of it by osmosis) and I'm hanging around with adults who don't seem to mind a schoolboy drenched in Old Spice tagging along. Plus, we're going to London for the day. I couldn't wait to see it.

I'm laughing as I remember this, because it was a complete disappointment. There was no sightseeing. Or fun of any sort. The conference might as well have been in Derby. We got into the hall, somewhere on the outskirts of London. It was like a big school hall with a stage at one end and a balcony at the other. The atmosphere was peculiar. I thought a conference would be like a big party and that there would a be a celebratory atmosphere. Nope. This place was deadly serious and it was full of some of the angriest people in Britain. Member after member took to the podium to rant about Blair. All the clichés were present: white guys with dreads, beardy blokes covered in badges, huge banners, flags of various countries (apart from the UK). I remember one guy in particular – he looked like Simon Bird (Will from *The Inbetweeners*) – ranting his head off on the stage. The crowd was loving it, he was smashing it. For his final flourish he called Tony Blair a Nazi and the whole hall cheered and then burst into

13

a rendition of 'Workers United Will Never Be Defeated', which I mumbled with as much gusto as John Redwood singing the Welsh national anthem.

At that precise moment I knew it was over. I'd made my decision. The anger was bad enough, but it was the delusion, however well meant some of it was. They truly believed that a revolution was imminent. I didn't and I thought, *If I know this at my age, how come they haven't figured it out?* That was one of the other lessons I learned early in politics: don't expect others to draw the same conclusions you do from the same experience. This is true of life too, of course, but in politics, success can be measured. Capitalism has not been overthrown.

A radical phase early in your political development is fairly common. That had been mine, and it was short-lived: I had lasted about three months. If that. At least I'd figured out early that I definitely wasn't on the hard left. I'd given it a good go but the anger, which at first had felt so energising, quickly became exhausting. It wasn't rooted in the real world. How can it be? Who on earth is angry all the time? Even bin Laden allowed himself the odd wank. Already, I'd had a powerful political education. I'd learned that socialism means vastly different things to different people. To some, like my mum, it was a byword for fairness. Her socialism was a gentle, poetic sort, rooted in tackling inequality and injustice. To others, like my former comrades in the SWP, socialism was something far bigger and more serious. It was about total control and it was rooted in heavy, serious texts. It was absolute. As well as attempting to tackle injustice by creating equality of outcome, it had pernicious implications for freedom of the media and judiciary, let alone opponents, internal or external.

I solemnly handed in my resignation. There was no raging row, no ice pick in the head. I don't know what the Nottingham equivalent of an ice pick in the head is – probably a chip cob in the face. A fate that, in retrospect, I'd have gleefully accepted.

At last, I turned fifteen and got my Labour Party membership card. The impact on my life was immediate. It was all I had in my wallet when getting ID'd once, so I handed it to the bouncer and tried my luck: 'You have to be eighteen to join the Labour Party, mate.' The bouncer slowly turned his head, raised an eyebrow and went, 'Yeah, I know. In you go.' Wow. I knew Labour wanted to give young people like me a better life, but this was incredible, I could use it as a fake ID. It was a magic pass into every pub and club in the city. What a perk. Some membership organisations throw in things like pet insurance or discounts at Homebase as an incentive. What good are they to an underage drinker without a pet or a need for a gazebo? This suited my needs perfectly.

I don't know how many pints I drank illegally with the help of that first Labour membership card, but I like to think that I might have drunkenly chatted politics with a stranger and got them to vote Labour. I like to think that because it's better than the truth. I probably bored hundreds of people stiff banging on about politics when they wanted to talk about something else. Still, it was all good preparation for some of my future gigs as a comedian.

My first experience of a Labour meeting was very different from my SWP ones. The people there were more civilised, they were more surprised to see a young person turn up and they were way more tedious. I presumed I was going to a meeting where we'd discuss things like education reform, the economy and the future of the NHS. What we actually discussed was bollards. Not a debate about the pros and cons of bollards, but a row between two councillors about where a set of bollards was located. One of them said they were on Main Street, the other said they were on King Street. It transpired that they were at a junction of the two streets, so they were technically on both. And anyway, who cares? Well, those two cared. They couldn't let it go. The meeting moved on to the next item on the agenda, but those two wouldn't stop. As everyone else tried to discuss something else, probably 'correspondence', one of them muttered under his breath 'Main Street' and then the other would mutter 'King Street'. These guys were old as well, easily in their seventies, and they were the most immature people at the meeting.

One thing did finally unite these two gladiators, though, and it was something I wasn't expecting. They hated the party leadership. Not in an SWP way, but they didn't trust the leadership of the party at all. That included everyone who worked for the party and anyone in a position of responsibility. The line that began the truce in the Battle of the Bollards was when 'Main Street' man referred to the leader as 'His Royal Blairness'. 'King Street' banged the table in assent. It still makes me laugh over twenty years later, because it's such a great insult. It's not nasty or rude. It even sounds like a compliment. But it's devastating sarcasm. The delivery was perfect as well, out of the side of the mouth, combined with a quick jerk of the head for extra emphasis and a flat Nottingham twang (if you're struggling to place the accent, imagine Vicky McClure from *Line of Duty* saying it). I realised I'd joined something far more complex than I'd bargained for. I was yet to appreciate the real factionalism in the party, but that first meeting was an introduction to a cynicism that elements of parties will always have about their leaders. However successful they might be.

Being a member of any party is what you make of it. At that stage I couldn't understand why you'd join but not join in. I wanted to go to every meeting possible, get out campaigning, absorb policy discussions and push leaflets through doors (as long as the houses didn't have a dog, as I didn't want my fingers to get bitten). By then, my mum, my sister and I had moved to the constituency of Broxtowe, which had a Labour MP for the first time since the 1950s. He was a lovely man called Nick Palmer, so when it was time to do work experience, I wrote and asked if I could do it with him. I don't know what the deal was at your school but most of my classmates seemed to be doing work experience at their parents' work. I don't think anyone had done work experience with an MP before. Understandable really – who'd want to? Me. I couldn't wait to peek inside the office of a Labour MP and be privy to high-level calls with ministers. To be in the loop about government business and find out what was really going on behind the scenes. A totally normal desire for a fifteen-year-old boy.

I was keen to learn and work hard. I knew I had to make a great first impression, as who knew where this might lead? I turned up on day one with an eyebrow missing. Well, not missing; I wasn't trying to find it. Some mates had shaved it off at a house party the previous weekend when I'd passed out, completely drunk. That Labour membership card was becoming a problem. Ever the optimist, I was grateful it wasn't worse. That said, had they shaved my pubes off, it's unlikely my MP would have noticed – even I didn't think it was going to go that well. My sister kindly drew on a replacement brow using a mascara brush. Her creation got more exotic as the week went on, and I ended up looking like Ru Paul.

I was off to a terrible start, nervous enough as it was without having to worry about my new colleagues thinking I'm some freak with an eyebrow that smudges. If they did notice, they were too kind to say anything to my mascara-covered face. I was straight in at the top, using my Machiavellian skills to alphabetise the filing cabinet and stuff some envelopes. None of it was very political, but I didn't care. I loved every small task because I felt it helped the bigger machine – a Labour government working to improve the lives of millions of people. I felt part of something. I'd found my political home.

Chapter 2

TRIBALISM

I can totally understand how people get radicalised. Being part of a tribe, particularly one formed with a mission in mind and a conviction of its own virtue, is highly seductive. That fusion of a moral purpose and a sense of belonging can inspire loyalty usually only reserved for family. It's something that unites churches, political parties and terrorist organisations. Obviously, I'm not likening my experience of working for the Labour Party to being part of a terror cell. Working for Labour was much worse. Say what you like about ISIS members, I bet their mobile phones work.

If you've worked in politics, you'll know what I mean. If you haven't, I accept that this all sounds very weird. Just think it through in increments. You start off believing the world is unequal or unfair. That's not so strange. You feel that you want to do something about it. A logical conclusion. You decide to join a mainstream political party with a history of campaigning for social justice. All makes sense so far. You get a job working for that party and doing everything you can to ensure it wins every election it stands in. Still sounds good. You think that anyone who disagrees with you has to be defeated. OK, it's starting to feel a bit combative, but let's see where this ends up. ANYONE WHO DISAGREES WITH ME IS EVIL AND MUST BE DESTROYED. Ah, you've gone too far, run the simulation again.

I never got to the final stage myself, but I definitely felt the pull of it. It's hard not to when politics in a democracy requires so many bloody elections. It becomes tiresome. You're in a permanent state of having to argue the case, beat your opponents and risk crushing defeat. It's a never-ending cycle. Any losses incurred aren't just a rejection of your efforts, they feel like a rejection of what you stand for. It's knackering so it's no wonder those who choose to expend so much physical and emotional energy have to be true believers. Who else would bother? When I reflect on it like this, it sounds like a Sisyphean hell. Many times it was, but it was also a riot. Working for Labour is one of the most thrilling, petrifying, rewarding and drunken things I've ever done.

Working for Labour was like being in the army. Apart from having to drive tanks. Oh, and shoot people (although there were times when I thought it might come to that). After working for a few MPs around Nottinghamshire for a couple of years, I got a job as a regional organiser for the Labour Party. I was based at the East Midlands regional office on the outskirts of Nottingham in a building called Harold Wilson House. It was a modern office building, reinforced with bars on the windows and security doors because the Countryside Alliance had tried to storm it during the debate on fox hunting. It lent the premises a military feel. The army analogy extended beyond the cosmetic, though. Over the next couple of years, I'd get sent all over the UK to work on various local election and by-election campaigns, often for months on end. These were like military tours, engaging with various enemies in different territories. I did it with glee, I wanted to be out there, but I suffered the political equivalent of post-Vietnam PTSD. I remember getting back from one campaign where I'd been stationed for three months and not knowing what to do with myself afterwards. I went to a supermarket for the first time in ages and found myself staring at an aisle of cereal like the bloke in *The Hurt Locker*.

By-elections are insane. They are the most intense political campaigns you will ever work on. Usually caused by a death or a resignation (which can then overshadow the whole thing), a by-election is where one seat is being contested outside of a general campaign. This means the entire machinery of each party is then focussed on one constituency of roughly 70,000 voters. The place gets bombarded with leaders, ministers, celebrities, media, activists and leaflets. I would hate to live somewhere having a parliamentary by-election because your phone will never stop ringing, your door will continually be knocked on and the sheer amount of direct mail you'll have to recycle will make you wonder about all parties' green credentials. They are British politics at its most aggressive, dishonest and tribal. I absolutely adored them.

My first taste of one was for Leicester South in 2004. It was like I'd never experienced politics before. It was the same feeling I had the first time I went to a boxing match. I couldn't believe it was allowed, but I loved it. The first thing I learned was that Labour activists absolutely hate the Liberal Democrats – and this was six years before the coalition government. They hate them more than the Tories. I was shocked; I thought the Lib Dems were sort-of Labour. The Tories had always seemed the more obvious enemy to me, and the Lib Dems more like harmless beardy lentil people. But that was before I'd ever had to fight a by-election against the bastards. Now, I should make it clear that I no longer feel this hostility towards the Lib Dems and have many friends in the party. If you are a Lib Dem, don't fear, I come in peace. Although I didn't back then. In a way, it's a sign of respect: the animosity was fuelled by their highly effective campaigning machine, which in short involved being more like the Tories in Tory areas and more like Labour in Labour areas. Not a bad idea, you might think, but it wasn't just that. It was the piety that accompanied it. The Lib Dems pretended to be meek and above it all, but they were the most cynical of the lot. It was like finding out Paddington Bear was a gun-runner. He must be nice, he's gentle and likes marmalade sandwiches. Jeremy Corbyn must have been taking notes.

The backdrop of the by-election wasn't just the death of the sitting MP, Jim Marshall, which caused it, but the Iraq War. Public anxiety was mounting, and Leicester South's constituency had a large Asian population. The Lib Dems were vocally anti-war. It was always going to be heated. The Tories couldn't win the seat and were breezing about the place treating the whole thing like a pre-season friendly. We bumped into them on the high street and they were like the Scottish at a World Cup – they were just happy to be there. I couldn't adjust to it. For Labour and the Lib Dems it was like an Old Firm title decider. The usual tensions were magnified by Iraq and the atmosphere of a by-election. The weird buzz you'd get when you were out campaigning and would see a rival party – in my case, the Lib Dems, the Tories, the Independents, the Respect Party and the Monster Raving Loonies (who were the most sensible ones of the lot) – was school fight-level adrenaline. The tension as you passed them on the same street – and we watched each other pass, like the Montagues and Capulets – was electrifying. Nothing would ever happen, of course, but you'd better believe I was prepared to run away if it did. Then you'd watch them to see if they were removing your leaflets from the letter boxes as they put their own in. A rule I learned very early: always shove the leaflet all the way through so that it can't be removed. Unless there's a big dog behind the door, in which case prioritise your fingers. Ultimately, it wasn't a dog that was to define my experience in Leicester South, but another animal.

You lose all sense of reason in a by-election. Whatever can be done for the cause must be done. You must be prepared to make the ultimate sacrifice. I guess what I'm trying to say is this: I dressed up as a chicken and stalked Charles Kennedy. Part of me felt bad as I was a fan of his. Another part of me thought it was fun – I was joining a select group of people who'd harassed a party leader dressed as a chicken. And another part of me wondered how a serious career in politics had culminated in me dressing as poultry.

The plan was, we'd find out where he was going to be and I'd have to drop whatever I happened to be doing at that point, get picked up by someone who had the chicken suit, quickly get changed behind a bush or a hedge and then creep up to Kennedy and get 'in shot' so that any media coverage about the Lib Dems' campaign was ruined.

The day arrived; I was in the middle of a door-knocking session when the call came through. The chicken suit turned up. It was that thick fake fur that fancy dress costumes are made of. It was boiling hot inside it, and it was the middle of summer. I couldn't see out of the rubber mask; the holes were tiny and I was sweating into my eyes. I had to keep cocking the chicken head back to peek out of the nostril hole. It would have been better to do it blindfolded.

With me in the suit we drove to where Kennedy was. I put on the mask and, as best as I could as I peeked out of the nostril, I waddled over. It took me ages to get to him as I was zigzagging around the street trying to see where I was going. Standing next to him wasn't enough, I had to cluck and flap like a chicken while a colleague of mine yelled into a loudhailer, 'Lib Dems, soft on crime, soft on thugs, soft on drugs!' over and over. I clucked and bobbed my head to the rhythm of the words. It felt like it went on for ages, it was shattering. Then it was over, and I had to walk back to the car, in a full chicken suit, drenched in sweat, drive back to the office and carry on organising leaflet rounds.

I've often wondered where I would have ended up had I carried on working in politics. The person with the loudhailer was Glenis Willmott, who went on to be leader of the Labour Party in the European Parliament, so maybe I'd have become a senior politician. As I watched that final day of the UK's involvement in the European Parliament years later, I wondered if Glenis ever wished it had been her in the chicken suit.

Labour lost in Leicester South and it still hurts me now. I was tribal because of my values, but I'd gone one further and acted on those beliefs, got involved and toiled for them. The intensity swelled inside me. I was more loyal than I was before. I hated my enemies more than I did before. I wanted to win more than before. I was completely invested in the success of the cause. The party's success was my success. If you've been an activist in any party or for any cause, you'll know exactly what I mean; it's not something unique to the Labour Party. If you haven't, I appreciate that this sounds like the ramblings of a cult member on a Netflix documentary. Don't worry, I never took part in any bizarre rituals, apart from dressing as a chicken. As well as all the important political lessons I learned working on a campaign in such ferocious circumstances, I also learned something about myself and what I enjoyed about politics. At that point in my life, I was as tribal as I've ever been and all I wanted to do was work on by-elections.

The thrill of battle is a great motivator but it's not enough on its own. You need to feel valued. New Labour was excellent at that. I was crushed after that defeat. I returned home after what felt like a year in a budget hotel and was completely flat. It's a bit like that sensation when you first get back from a festival or a holiday: normal life feels cruelly dull after such intensity. Even worse, it felt like it had all been for nothing.

However, there was a silver lining. Good leaders and bosses understand the toil such a defeat takes on you and realise that there must be reward for the effort. Being the party of government comes with a great perk – you can throw parties at Downing Street. Going to Number 10 at any time was a treat; going there for a party was even better. The invite came through the post, on thick white card with embossed black letters on it: *The prime minister requests the company of Mr Matthew Forde.* I wasn't going to turn down such a polite request.

We got the train down from Nottingham, trying to act like going to Number 10 was the most normal thing in the world. Queuing up to get through the big gates at the bottom, I couldn't believe they were actually going to let me in. They checked my ID and I was allowed to saunter up Downing Street at my leisure. That was the coolest bit and I tried to savour every step. I'd stood at the gates before and tried in vain to see the front door. Now I was there, approaching that imposing black door, with its beautiful shiny black gloss. The letter box, the lamp above the door, even the font of the number '10' – everything about it looks great. It's the backdrop to so many important moments in history. We went through that famous door, ascended the staircase past the portraits of previous prime ministers and into a series of reception rooms where we marvelled at a stunning sight: a load of Labour staff getting smashed on Stella. *Oh my God, it's a free bar. Not again.*

You see, I'd been to Number 10 before with my mate Pete for a Young Labour reception a couple of years previously. We'd got so drunk we'd had to prop ourselves up on the mantelpiece to stand up straight, but then furiously tried to sober up on the only food they had – carrot batons – as Tony Blair entered. Meeting the prime minister is an honour; meeting him in his house while drunk is like a cheese dream, and I was living it. However, I'd drunk so much free Stella I was busting for the toilet. I left Pete clinging to that mantelpiece and legged it down the stairs before Blair started working the room.

I'm tempted to pretend that I can't remember what I said the first time I actually got to meet the prime minister. But I can. My exact words were, 'Excuse me, mate, do you know where the bogs are?' In my defence, I didn't realise it was Tony Blair because he had his back to me. He turned around and I blurted, 'Oh God, it's you, I'm so sorry.' Then, showing the mark of true leadership, the most powerful man in the country told me where the toilets were. I don't know if you've been briefed by a prime minister on the nearest safe place to piss, but I highly recommend it.

If I loved fighting our external opponents, I felt very differently about fighting our internal ones. It was draining and depressing. Every major party has this problem because they're just too big to be one tribe. They are a coalition of several tribes and always have been. Internal ideological differences can have their benefits:

when things are going well, it can look like a party is dynamic and brimming with ideas. When times are bad, it exposes the truth – parties are bitterly divided and contain an unhealthy number of people who would happily sabotage their own party's success. That's why the boundaries have to be clearly defined and enforced. Internal debate and dissent are vital but if the tent is too big, it will end up containing those who want to burn the tent down. My experience was a Labour one so that's the only one I'm qualified to talk about.

Whatever political tradition you come from, I hope we all agree that political parties should seek to win elections. You may wonder why I even mention it; it should not be a controversial view. Sadly, in my experience, in some Labour Party meetings it was. I still meet Labour members who would rather be ideologically pure than be in government. Those people, however well-meaning they may think they are, do not belong in the Labour Party. An impartial observer might be tempted to conclude that both sides are as bad as each other, that the hard left rebelled against Blair and then the Blairites rebelled against the hard left. But it's only the hard left who view victory as a compromise. By their own admission, they are not invested in the electoral success of the party. No school in its right mind would employ a teacher who says, 'I don't think pupils should be passing exams, I'd rather teach them stuff that's not on the curriculum and have them fail.'

That's why I found it so frustrating in the Labour Party, because one side is trying to subvert the reason Labour was founded in the first place – to win elections. As someone who'd grown up in desperate need of a Labour government, the indulgence of our internal opponents baffled and angered me. Once we were out of office, we wouldn't be able to help the most vulnerable people in society, and what was Labour about if not that?

The hard left is riddled with contradictions. They claim to care more about the vulnerable, yet they deliver Tory victories every time they're in charge of the party. They claim to hate the Tory party more than anyone, yet they do more to help it win than anyone else. The contradiction that is the most pernicious, but the one that tickles me the most, is the suggestion that they are morally superior to their opponents. They masquerade as gentle pacifists, yet they are some of the angriest people you'll ever encounter. They really do belong in the SWP. If you've never been to a Labour meeting before and had to guess which person was going to be the most aggressive in the room, I bet you wouldn't pick the right one. You might go for the young guy in the Fred Perry shirt. Or the serious-looking middle-aged woman. Well, you'd be wrong. It's Beardy Old Guy every time. He'll even smile at you on the way in. Then once the meeting starts, BANG! He's off. It's like something out of a *Men in Black* film where an evil shapeshifting alien warlord chooses the form of a cute old lady because she's the last person they'd expect to be the baddie. If the hard left were as committed to a world of respect and peace as they say they are, they'd start at home and treat their opponents in the party with the love and compassion they preach about.

Labour's relationship with its own history is disastrous. A view has been allowed to take hold that the left of the party is 'real' Labour and that the right of the party are imposters who don't really hold Labour values. During my time there, I was on the right of the party for two key reasons:

- The right of the party more closely reflected my opinions and, I believe, the values of the country.
- People from my background needed a Labour government and the right of the party, being more in tune with the country, was the most likely to win.

So, what are the values of the right of the party that I found so appealing? Based on my experience of growing up around all sorts of petty crime and intimidation, New Labour being tough on crime was massive. When I was a kid, our house was burgled. We went to Skegness for the week to stay in a caravan and came back to find our house raided. Everything was gone, apart from the heavy furniture. We had our suspicions about who might have done it, but they were never caught – not enough fingerprints and no CCTV. I still prickle at the powerlessness of getting burgled. Being burgled isn't about the theft, it's the thought of a bully prowling around your home, violating your space. There's nothing left wing about letting people get intimidated in a home they can't afford to move out of. That burglary (and subsequent ones) had a huge impact on my politics.

I remember a discussion about crime at a Labour meeting in a leafier part of Nottingham many years later. Most of the members felt that expanding CCTV coverage was an infringement of civil liberties. I asked if any of them had been burgled. None of them had. There is a legitimate debate to be had about civil liberties and I care about them deeply, but in my experience those who focussed on the apparent evils of CCTV had never needed to rely on it after being the victims of crime. I just wanted the criminals to get caught, I wasn't advocating the guillotine. Although I would fantasise about it. I mean, these people even stole my MC Hammer album, one of the most brazen crimes you can commit. The cover even states 'U Can't Touch This'.

Crime was personal for me, but it wasn't the only reason I was more in tune with New Labour than those further to the left. While I believed in the power of the state to tackle inequalities in health and education and to keep us safe, I didn't want it to run everything. Not only did I think it would be economically inefficient, advocates of state control struggle to produce examples of planned economies where life is better than under a form of regulated capitalism. That was my philosophical starting point; plus, my experience in the SWP had made me wary of people who idolised Lenin and Stalin. You might expect it in fringe parties but celebrating authoritarians and dictators is a kink that mainstream parties shouldn't tolerate. The Soviet Union is like catnip to swathes of the Labour Party who can happily overlook the tens of millions dead, the gulags, the secret police, the violent suppression of dissent, the lack of a free media, free judiciary or democracy because, er, they were lefties. The left, like the right, is a big space and parts of it are absolutely revolting and shouldn't be defended out of misplaced tribal loyalty. People with facial hair might as well support Harold Shipman because he had a beard.

The fight can be addictive, but you have to remember what you're fighting for. That's why it's so important to be clear about what you think and to constantly reassess your analysis.

Chapter 3

IDEOLOGY, PRINCIPLES AND MINDSET

Politics is a great creative adventure to solve the problems we face as a society with good ideas, but how often is it thought of like that? The combative nature of politics often distracts us from enjoying the intellectual challenge of engaging with a party's ideas or coming up with our own. We tend to pick a side and then leave it at that, having reached our conclusion, satisfied that we've done all the political thinking we need to do. But we limit our understanding as well as our enjoyment of politics if we don't try and continually engage with new and differing ideas, including those we disagree with. Whether it's big ideas (ideologies, the relationship between the citizen and the state, the notion of freedom) or policy ideas (Right to Buy, the minimum wage, free schools), entertaining new ideas is the fuel of politics. And what happens if you run out of fuel? Well, depending on the scenario, you either come to a juddering halt on the motorway and have to call the AA or you can't heat your home. Even worse, it might mean you can't fire up the BBQ. It's no way to live.

I feel conflicted about ideology in the same way I feel conflicted about religion. They're both ways of understanding the world and of letting others know, in shorthand, what your outlook on life is. They can inspire human beings to make huge sacrifices for the greater good. They can sustain communities for generations, giving them a focus and moral purpose. They can help promote cultures of kindness and love. But. But, but, but. They can breed dogmatism, fanaticism and a hatred of non-believers. Most people don't get involved in a church to do harm, they get involved to do some good and to socialise with like-minded people. It's the same with politics. And with both, it's up to you how far you go. The ideology you subscribe to can be a broad theme that you loosely agree with, or it can be an absolute set of rules that cannot be deviated from. You can be comfortable with other people having a different world view without presuming them to be morally reprehensible. You can interpret sacred texts, whether it's the Bible or Labour's 2019 manifesto, as illustrative stories or you can take them completely literally. For instance, Jesus healing the blind could be a metaphor about him enlightening people, rather than literally making blind people see. Jeremy Corbyn's promise to nationalise the UK's entire broadband infrastructure and give it to everyone for free clearly shouldn't have been taken literally, it should have been seen as a metaphor for, well, I don't know . . . But it shouldn't have been taken literally.

For the entire time that I considered myself a socialist – that is, well into my twenties – I was embarrassingly proud of it. I say embarrassingly because that would be true of any fervent affiliation to a political label, not just socialism. I wore it as a mark of who I was. To be fair, it was a bit of a muted pride after I witnessed the toxic internal party shenanigans. To give you an idea of scale, let's say it was just above that of a grandparent who maintains a well-tended garden, but well below that of an Audi owner. Of course, you want to feel good about your guiding political philosophy, but there can be a sense of superiority when you decide what you think is the 'right way'. It can take time to finesse your thinking and realise that, although you still believe yourself to be correct, your opponents just have a different perspective to you based on different experiences which have led them to different conclusions. They're not evil. Well, not all of them.

When you first engage with your preferred political philosophy, you can be remarkably unquestioning about its shortcomings. For years, I used socialism as a byword for fairness. I naively thought they were completely interchangeable. I thought calling myself a socialist showed that I cared about injustice and wanted to do something about it. I enjoyed reading about Marx, Lenin and Luxemburg, but I didn't feel connected to them. So why didn't this make me question if I was a socialist or not? Because it didn't feel like the same thing. It was a simple British socialism I was into, not the bloodthirsty Russian stuff. It wasn't socialism as a rigid economic doctrine about planned economies that hooked me, it was about using the power of the state to give disadvantaged people a fair start in life. It was a traditional Labour view of socialism, committed to democracy and not revolution, giving a voice to the voiceless and, crucially, equality of opportunity not equality of outcome. In reality I am, and always was, a social democrat, because I believe that the market has a role to play in society. It took me a long time to realise it. Maybe it's because 'social democrat' sounds less exciting. It's like getting into punk and then finding out you prefer Ed Sheeran. Hang on a minute, no, that's too extreme an example, it's nowhere near as bad as that.

There's a paradox about political education. You open yourself up to a vast garden of thinkers, ideas and books, but if you're not careful, they're all just fertilising your own beliefs. You can end up becoming more aware and educated about your chosen side, but also closing yourself off to alternatives. You're simultaneously becoming more enlightened and more ignorant. We do this with other areas of our lives, of course, so we shouldn't feel too bad about it. I have the same thing every time I go to Wagamama: chicken katsu curry. It's the perfect dish. Don't @ me. I've occasionally experimented and had something else, usually due to peer pressure, and I have always regretted it, my night is ruined and I'm chuntering into my Asahi until I go home. Only consuming one strand of political thought is even worse, it would be like eating chicken katsu curry for every meal, all day every day. Now, at first that might sound like a treat, like a child who fantasises about only ever eating Big Macs. But you'll bloat up, feel nauseous and end up being sick on yourself. Yes, I realise

36

I've made my point and this metaphor is getting out of control. I'll move on.

I will just say this about chicken katsu curry, though – I reckon I could go a long time having it for breakfast, dinner and tea. A few months at least. Anyway, like I say, I'll move on.

I think it's the mix of textures and flavours. It's not a bag of ready-salted crisps. It's spicy, it's tangy, it's crispy, it's soft, it's got a bit of a kick but not too much. It goes great with lager. You're right, though, this hasn't got anything to do with politics, so I'll leave it there.

It is amazing, though.

God, I really want one now.

You probably do too now, I'm so sorry.

It can be difficult and sometimes infuriating but being open to opposing views is healthy and helps your thinking develop in a more rounded way. We all prefer to read books about people and ideas we like, but I would recommend trying each year to read a couple about an opposing philosophy or by a politician from the other side. The main benefit is that it demystifies your opponents. It's easy to develop assumptions of bad faith, so the primary gain is a lowering of the anxiety about the motives of people you disagree with. You get an insight into their thinking and realise it's not because they want to ruin everything; they just have a different perspective based on a different experience. The other effect is that it challenges you to interrogate yourself, which leads to one of two possible outcomes: either you change your mind, which is always oddly pleasurable, or you improve your existing position by testing it. Whether it's Adam Smith's *The Wealth of Nations* or Edwina Currie's *Diaries*, make the effort to expose yourself to other points of view on a regular basis.

Ideologies give you a quick way to make sense of the world. They give you an easy answer to a problem without the need for nuance. If you're a capitalist, you'll tend to favour less state involvement. So, whatever the problem, the first answer is to deregulate or privatise. If you're a socialist, your first instinct will be to regulate more or nationalise. If you're a libertarian, your first instinct is probably that people should be allowed to do heroin wherever they want.

In one way, sticking to an ideology means you're consistent. You have a clear view about the role of the state and in any given scenario, your solution fits with your guiding philosophy. But there are many problems with this. The first is that it's lazy. You don't need to engage with the detail of what could be a complex problem and you're not considering the context at all. In fact, you don't even need to be told anything about the issue, you always know what your answer will be. The second problem is that life is complicated. Political problems profoundly affect people's lives and they exist not in isolation as an intellectual exercise, but often in difficult or exceptional circumstances.

Take the UK government furlough scheme during the coronavirus pandemic in 2020. A Conservative government decided to effectively pay the public's wages to prevent the economy from collapsing. That in itself is astonishing enough. Leave aside the fact that it was the right thing to do economically, let alone morally; it was a big answer to a big problem. I think most of us were surprised that any government, let alone the Tories, would do something so radical. But let's see how you feel if you remove the context and consider whether, in general, you'd support the state paying people's wages. If you're a capitalist, it's likely that you'd be absolutely against it. Even if you're not, you're still probably against it. But the context changes things. This wasn't 'in general', this was during a global public health crisis when a lethal virus meant that economic activity around the world was severely restricted. Without that money paid directly into people's pockets, an unprecedented economic collapse would have caused financial and social chaos. Even worse, we might have completely run out of chicken katsu curry. In that situation, responsible capitalists recognised the need for state intervention. It doesn't mean they've changed their minds and are now convinced that the state should always do this, it's about being flexible when appropriate.

You can develop your thinking easily. Take the principle of freedom and consider how it relates to our view of the state. If we see the state as a repressive force, it's because we believe the government restricts our freedoms – like the freedom to smoke indoors or drive without a seat belt. If we see the state as an enabling force, we believe the state creates freedoms – like the freedoms created by a high-quality state education system or the freedom to live in peace thanks to the rule of law and policing. Of course, it's possible to believe all those things – that the smoking ban was illiberal but that the state should provide free, high-quality education. Thinking these things through issue by issue gives us a deeper insight into our own opinions, rather than just using our ideology as a crutch. It also reminds us that different policy areas require different answers and that there's nothing wrong with advocating state intervention in some areas, like crime, and not advocating it in others, like limiting how much chocolate you can eat. Maybe that's just personal to me.

Once you've figured out what your values and principles are, you need to keep your thinking updated. Nostalgia is a killer. So many politicians and activists just want to repeat the past. We've all met them – Brexiteer Tories obsessed with World War II, the hard left obsessed with the 1970s, Blairites who still think it's 1997. OK, now you mention it, nostalgia isn't all bad. However, there's a distinction to be made. Remembering the good old days is a part of the human condition. It's normal and pleasurable to reminisce, particularly if it's about rare victories. The danger in politics is that our nostalgia for the time gets fused with a desire to repeat it identically. In policy terms, that means irrelevance. Think of it like this: you loved the Thatcher era and agreed with the privatisation of British Rail. It got privatised. So, what are you going to do now in the 2020s, advocate privatising it again? British Rail doesn't exist anymore. If you want to improve rail travel in the future, you'll need to come up with a new answer that reflects the modern reality.

Ultimately, it's about having the right mindset. Explore and enjoy the ideology but not at the expense of it being relevant. Sometimes I worry that those who bury themselves in complex political philosophy, as important as knowledge is, are doing it as an alternative to engaging with reality. They're becoming ideological hermits, pursuing politics in a way that doesn't enrich debate or enhance society. In short, know your values but don't strive for purity or you'll end up down a dead end. Once you're down a dead end there's only one way to go and that's reverse out. Actually, there is another option, you can keep going for a bit, but you will crash the car. What a great metaphor for the Labour Party.

Chapter 4

THE POWER OF INDIVIDUALS

Politics attracts strange people. Standing for office is exposing. Being in office is exhausting. Losing office is humiliating. Who'd want to do it? Well, the answer is egotists, fantasists, misfits, sociopaths, nerds and berks. I was definitely in the final category. However, amidst the Addams Family-type freaks you find there, there are also some of the world's most inspirational people. Some are more visible than others – leaders like Barack Obama – but at every level you will find some of the most motivated, caring, resilient and impressive individuals in society. It might be an odd way to think about it, but at certain times, we live vicariously through our leaders. If they are good prime ministers or presidents, our lives are enhanced. Their decisions will help determine how healthy and how wealthy we are. We place on their backs our hopes and dreams as if they are personally in charge of our future.

Tony Blair blew me away. Which sounds like a *Daily Star* headline. But he did. (Not in a *Daily Star* way.) Until he came along, I thought politicians were either nasty (Thatcher) or dull (Major – although it turns out not as dull as we thought, the dirty dog). The Tories' final term had been a sleaze-drenched nightmare. They were completely out of ideas and totally out of tune with the country. Labour winning in 1997 was like that bit in *Beauty and the Beast* where the spell has been lifted and colours burst through the foreboding castle, bringing it back to life. You remember the scene: the candelabra became a person, the footstool became a dog, the portly talking clock became John Prescott and started punching people.

That election didn't just feel like a choice between two political parties, it felt like a choice between two completely different styles. The Conservatives were tired, negative and unpleasant. Labour were young, positive and optimistic. Labour had finally won, which to me was particularly huge as I'd only ever known a Conservative government. Any victory would have been brilliant, but a victory on the scale that Blair achieved, taking Labour from eighteen years in the wilderness to a 179-seat majority, was and still is incredible. It's the closest thing to a revolution you can get in a democracy. It's like the day Germany beat Brazil 7–1 at the World Cup. Pubs fell silent with every extra goal. You didn't need to support either side, everyone knew they were witnessing something momentous. Just like old World Cup goals, I'll still watch highlights of the 1997 election on YouTube when I'm drunk. I'll wake up in bed at 5 a.m. to find the laptop on, playing old Blair speeches. I think my girlfriend would rather I watched pornography.

The victories were only part of the reason I was so inspired by him. He was obviously talented. He could think clearly and speak simply but with passion. He still has the ability to make his opinion in any debate sound like the most rational and least political position possible. His temperament was exceptional, which expressed itself in three ways. It meant he rarely ever made verbal gaffes. Think of the politicians we have today and imagine them having that ability. Perhaps more importantly, it meant that he never lost his temper or was rude to anyone – in private or in public. On top of that, he clearly liked people and it showed. In turn, people liked him. Leaders need to get things done, and you can only do that if you can win people over. So many politicians seem allergic to the public, in part frightened by them, in part repelled by them. There's a reason he was applauded out of the House of Commons by MPs on all sides – it was because of his success and achievement, but also because he was always polite and treated people with courtesy. That's not always the way in politics and if you disagree with me, you can piss off. See, it's almost impossible.

Intellect and common human decency are crucial, but leaders require something else and Blair has tons of it: charisma. Charisma on its own is in danger of being shallow but when combined with those other talents, it can help change the world. It can unlock negotiations, win over new allies and keep your own side energised. The people we choose to lead us as a nation should be impressive individuals. After all, it's the biggest job in the country – they represent us to the whole world. As part of the backlash against Blair, particularly on the left, there was a snobbery around charisma as a desirable quality. This was a way of acknowledging his charisma but turning it into a negative. It was also because the hard left couldn't find anyone who was charismatic to lead them, so they had to pretend that it didn't matter. Great idea – let's go through a democratic exercise that requires inspiring millions of people and let's pick someone barely capable of motivating their own cat. Which I realise would be quite a tough task as cats are moody little buggers. But you get the point.

All that natural ability would count for nothing in politics if it wasn't used to deliver significant change. Tony Blair and his government transformed the country for the better and that's ultimately why I rated him so much. He put his abilities to the service of the nation and improved millions of lives in the process. Sound economic management helped create the longest period of growth in UK history. The receipts of that growth were poured into schools, delivering the best ever GCSE and A Level results we'd had, and into hospitals, leading to record cuts in waiting times for hospital treatment. More police on the streets helped cut crime in half, keeping people safer in their homes. ASBOs, mocked by elements of the media, gave communities blighted by crime the power to take action against the bullies. Blair removed the homophobic Section 28 which prevented the teaching of homosexuality in schools, delivered peace in Northern Ireland, devolution in Scotland and Wales, used a windfall tax on the privatised utilities to help cut youth unemployment, gave the UK its first ever minimum wage and new tax credits which helped redistribute wealth and opportunity. I didn't even have to google that, it's just in there and always will be, along with whatever other rubbish I've remembered at the expense of useful information, like old football shirt sponsors and the opening words of the *A-Team* theme tune.*

It was by far the best government I've lived under. It was progressive, principled and open. It transformed the life chances of millions of people, especially people from my sort of background. What a tragedy then that at the age of thirty-seven, I have only lived under a progressive government for thirteen years of my life. And yes, they were the New Labour years before you mutter something sarcastic to yourself.

I can't talk about Tony Blair's legacy without mentioning Iraq. Don't worry, I'm not about to rehearse the arguments for and against the invasion. I just think it's sad that it's so rare to find a balanced view on it. The intelligence that led to the war was catastrophically awful and it's right to conclude that we can never go to war on such flimsy proof ever again. But it's also possible to come to a more sympathetic conclusion about Blair's motives. We'd been to war with Saddam before and he'd repeatedly frustrated the work of UN weapons inspectors, and had possessed WMD and used chemical weapons in the past. Inaction would also have come at a price. Look at what happened in Syria. When Assad launched a chemical attack on his own people,

---

* I'd planned to quote the words from the start of *The A-Team* in a pathetic attempt to impress you. Sadly, I'm not legally allowed to reproduce them. Which is a problem no-one can help me with.

Ed Miliband got his MPs to vote against military action and the West stood by. Look at the state of Syria now and look who has been emboldened there. We've left that place to the mercy of Assad, Putin and ISIS and it's the people of Syria who have suffered. I guess what I'm saying is that always seeing opposition to military action as the morally superior choice is deeply flawed. Walking by on the other side of the street should also be considered irresponsible. We don't discuss Syria in the same way that we discuss Iraq. Given how toxic the Iraq debate has become, maybe that's a good thing, but having a lopsided moral judgement on intervention means we're in danger of learning the wrong lessons. It's not that it's never our business, it's that in future before we commit troops we need accurate intelligence, better planning and the commitment to stay as long as it takes. I doubt I've changed your mind on the matter but at least writing this in a book means I can't hear you if you are screaming back at me through a loudhailer. If you are doing that right now, fair play for committing to it. Anyway, the Iraq War isn't exactly a fertile ground for mega LOLs, so let's move on.

It would be unfair to give all the credit for the New Labour government to Tony Blair. His administration consisted of a collection of some exceptional talents. Gordon Brown was central to its appeal and a hugely inspirational figure. He was a very different orator to Blair and moved an audience in a different way. Brown had an inherent moral clout, an earthiness that lent his speeches a biblical rumble. They felt like they should have been delivered against a dramatic background of rain, thunder and lightning. Most of what's written about Blair and Brown focusses on their differences of opinion, but they were united on so much and together achieved major milestones – like cancelling the debt of the world's poorest countries. They complemented each other perfectly: Blair the charismatic front man, Brown the economic anchor. Then there was Mo Mowlam, Alistair Darling, Alan Johnson, Margaret Beckett, Jack Straw, Patricia Hewitt, Harriet Harman, Robin Cook, Peter Mandelson, David Blunkett, John Reid, Hilary Benn . . . It was like a fantasy team of political heavyweights. I still have the signed photos I collected of them as a teenager.

In later years one Labour figure in particular would come to mean more to me than any of them and in a way that I would never have guessed.

Tessa Jowell was magical. There's no other way to describe her. She was completely unlike any other person I've ever met. Trying to explain what made her so special would be like trying to describe a new colour. If you were lucky enough to meet her, then you'll have felt her uniqueness. An almost holy presence, she had an immediate calming effect on a room. If I were still a religious person, I'd say that I'd met a saint. I don't go in for all the hippy stuff about chakras and energy, but she had an aura about her that was like a spell. It was like she had a charisma all of her own. She made you behave better just by being there. It was a gentle authority, not one of judgement or severity, but one that appealed to your better instincts and made you want to be more like her. I realise this might all feel a bit over the top, so let me reassure you: I wasn't on any drugs of any sort when I met her, and I was completely sober.

I first met Tessa in 2014 when I interviewed her in front of an audience for my podcast, *The Political Party* (hit subscribe and leave a nice iTunes review, please). It's the episode I get asked about the most and here's why. No one has ever talked about being a politician in the way Tessa did. It captured her personality perfectly in a way that routine media interviews never could. Everyone who's heard that episode knows they heard someone special. She started talking about how much being a politician meant to her. The responsibility her constituents had placed in her was something she valued way beyond a validation of her politics. I could see as she was describing this that she was becoming emotional, and when she said that it was an honour to represent people in Parliament, her eyes began to glisten. The room was completely silent; everyone in the audience was leaning forward, feeling themselves drawn to her. The spectators were getting something they hadn't expected and they were hooked. They'd come out to see some stand-up comedy followed by a light-hearted interview with a bit of serious politics thrown in (see, it's really got everything. Hit subscribe and leave a 5-star review on iTunes). And here they now were, totally entranced by her, some of them getting emotional too.

I think about that moment a lot and I think about Tessa a lot too. In the years since she tragically died, politics has become coarser. It's almost as if she was single-handedly holding back the tide of anger and bigotry and now that she's gone, it's taken over. I know that's not true and I know that there are many other wonderful and decent people in many parties, but Tessa was extra special and we could really do with her now. You'll have to forgive me, I think I've got something in my eye.

Being an elected politician requires a resilience that very few possess. While it is rewarding, it is also draining, humiliating and lonely. Even those of us who've worked in politics never really get close to that feeling of isolation. When it's your name on the posters and it's you standing in a council leisure centre at 3 a.m., surrounded by grinning opponents waiting to find out if you've been fired by public vote as the whole country watches, it's a lonely job and any defeat will feel personal. Would you want to do it? Well, you're reading this book so you might, and I don't want to put you off, but standing for public office, even in a safe seat for a council election, is an exposing exercise. It takes guts to submit yourself and your opinions to public judgement and ridicule. Things are rarely easy, and every decision and every action has a potential downside. In fact, that was one of many important political lessons I learned early on, when I first got a job working for an MP.

Paddy Tipping was the MP for Sherwood. You might recognise the name as he'd been minister for the millennium bug, which surprised anyone who knew him because he barely knew how to send an email. He was tall, bearded and looked like he'd been a runner when he was young. He had a soft, deep voice and a big booming laugh. Whatever he was doing, he would be totally immersed in it and loving every minute of it. He was impossible to dislike, because he embodied the perfect combination of humanity, empathy, wit and warmth.

God knows what he saw in me and why he took me on, but I started to do a couple of days a week in his constituency office. This wasn't an oak-panelled Westminster introduction to working in politics, this was a room above a council office in Nottinghamshire introduction to working in politics. The constituency was a semi-rural mixture of former pit villages and some posh estates. I loved it. Mainly because the office was on Hucknall high street, which had about fifteen bakeries on it. One of which made chicken balti pasties for 60p. I was in politics and curry pasty heaven.

Paddy taught me so much, and not just about the importance of having an office near a load of bakeries. In keeping with his personality, the first thing I learned from Paddy was the power of positivity. He understood that contrary to some wisdom, positive messages are more powerful than negative messages, and I saw this work in front of audiences. I remember a town hall hustings in the early 2000s where Paddy was on stage against his opponents from the other parties. That day the local paper's front-page headline was something like *WARNING: LIVING IN HUCKNALL CAN DAMAGE YOUR HEALTH, YOUR WEALTH AND YOUR HAPPINESS* about a survey apparently showing how poorly local services were performing. The first thing the panel was asked was for their reaction to this study. Each one of them took turns talking tough about the yobs who ruin the area, about litter in the park, the stuff you'd expect them to say. Each one of them got a decent round of applause. Paddy went last and took a completely different tack. 'You know what?' he said. 'I'm sick of people talking this area down. I'm proud of the teachers in our local schools and I'm proud of the coppers trying to keep us safe.' It went off. The applause was deafening and the outpouring of positivity from the audience said it all.

But it wasn't just a lesson about optimism, it was a lesson about place. Most people want to be proud of where they live. Many of them can't afford to move so if you're constantly trashing an area, you're trashing the people who live there. It doesn't mean they're not realistic or animated about problems they face, it means that the language you use when you address their issues is profoundly important. If I'd have been Paddy, I'd have gone further and added a line about 'being proud of the local bakeries that sell chicken balti pasties for just 60p', but you can't have everything.

Paddy was a campaigning MP. He behaved every day as if the election was taking place tomorrow. He would use any excuse to produce a leaflet on some topic or other. On Mother's Day, he'd stand on the high street with a load of roses and hand them out to mums who were pushing prams or walking their kids. He produced a Mother's Day card that inside told them all the things Labour was doing for families. It was a brilliant way to deliver a message and cheer people up. He'd pull similar stunts at Christmas, Easter and any other significant day. I think we even did stuff around the FA Cup Final about what Labour was doing for grassroots sport. It's a good job this was before things like Movember and Veganuary took off or he'd have been out there now handing out free beard oil and Labour-branded tofu.

Most political leaflets are awful and even if they're half decent, they don't get read. Paddy would dream up ingenious ways to get his name into people's homes, such as making a calendar with helpful local phone numbers on for people to put on their fridge so that all year round his face was in their kitchens. He was all about the photos. I'm still amazed by politicians who put out a leaflet that consists of blocks of endless text and three photos of them looking stiff and glum outside a police station, a school and a hospital. All in the same clothes, so they'd clearly done it all in the same day. In any event, what good is a photo of an MP standing side by side with a copper, both staring at the camera? Paddy would always get photos of him chatting to the people he was pictured with. Sometimes, if they were nervous, he'd just go, 'We're chatting, aren't we? We're chatting,' and they'd answer, 'Yeah, we're chatting, Paddy.' And then he'd say, 'We are as well, we're chatting,' and then they'd come back with, 'Oh yes, we're chatting, all right,' and it would carry on and that's all they'd say to each other. I'd be snapping away, and the photos would make it look like they were old pals having the time of their lives. Genius.

He applied the same zeal he had for campaigning to ensuring that incidents and grievances were addressed and sorted out. All week we'd consume the local media to see what was happening. If there'd been a spate of burglaries or antisocial behaviour in a local park, we'd go to wherever the issue was and knock on every door so that residents could speak to Paddy about it. He would always have a stack of letters with him so that anyone who was out would get one through the door explaining he'd come round to talk about the problems with the park, for example, and giving them his number if they wanted to tell him anything. Then he'd get the police and local council involved and after that, write back to them all individually. I've never known an MP to be so proactive. What a service.

He was fearless, too. I knocked on one door once, a bloke opened it and I was halfway through explaining that I was here with the local MP when this man stopped me and said, 'It's a good job he didn't knock on my door himself or I'd have sparked the fucker out.' I said goodbye and told Paddy it was a good job he hadn't knocked on the door for the reason the bloke had given. Paddy didn't miss a beat; he went straight to the door and knocked on it. I thought all hell was going to break loose and braced myself to have to intervene. Within a minute, though, he had this bloke roaring with laughter. People talk about Derren Brown and Dynamo. The best mind tricks I ever saw were performed by Paddy Tipping, MP for Sherwood. Not the best stage name – maybe that's why he stuck to politics.

One of the consequences of all this was that the people of Sherwood felt they had an MP who was very visible. They always knew where he was if they needed him. Political management is all about communication. If in doubt, make sure you're regularly talking to your audiences – whether it's members, other politicians or voters. As any MP quickly discovers, you need to keep other local politicians on your own side at bay. A few of them will be after your job. You've got to keep them close so that they don't start organising against you. Councillors are the worst for it. All week they're in a group together while the MP is in Parliament. The distance can build mistrust if you're not careful, and some of them will be hostile regardless of your efforts. From what I could tell, Paddy kept what could have been a deeply rebellious group of old-school Labour councillors onside via a mixture of hard work, regular contact and, most importantly, beer.

Never underestimate the power of the pint. Paddy made campaigning fun. He'd have teams out door-knocking and leafletting every Saturday, even when a general election was four years away. No one in that constituency could say they never saw their MP. Afterwards we'd all go straight to the pub. Then there were the local party meetings, often held in pubs, and fundraisers in pubs and clubs on top of that. It was like being in a band. Every Saturday we'd be in a different venue that I'd leave half-cut. This all sounds basic but there are so many MPs who don't do any of this. Either they think they're above it, they can't be bothered or they're intimidated by their local members. Some of them have every right to be, but if you're the MP it's on you to take the lead and nurture those relationships. Don't get me wrong, I'm not saying that the secret to political success is to get everyone bladdered but . . . Well, maybe I am, but what I really mean is if you make a point of being visible and approachable and you're always communicating, you earn goodwill and respect. From some people . . .

No matter how popular and likeable you are, there will always be groups you'll never please. Paddy was one of the most prominent MPs campaigning against fox hunting. This meant the Countryside Alliance were gunning for him. Given that a fair few of their members actually have guns, it did start to get a bit serious. The first warning was a deck of cards they produced, similar to the one the US army had done in Iraq, with each playing card featuring one of Britain's 'most prejudiced MPs'. Paddy was one of them. We had the card on a pinboard in the office somewhere and it seemed like a bit of a joke. Then the phone calls started. We were used to answerphone messages left at about half eleven at night from the occasional drunk, but these were left in the early hours of the morning by a very stern man.

I can recall one of them word for word. You'd hear the bleep of the answerphone and then his voice though gritted teeth. 'I've got a message for Paddy Tipping. He says he'd like to ban hunting. Well, I'd like to cut his beard off. With a rusty knife. Freedom to hunt!' I'm not sure if I was meant to laugh, but I did. What a crap threat. 'I'm going to cut your beard off.' I suppose the rusty knife bit sounds a bit uncomfortable, but it's hardly waterboarding. What are you going to do next, iron my trousers for me, with a cold iron? It never got to Paddy and he didn't seem to take it personally. How could he? The most he was being threatened with was a cheap makeover. Anyway, I'd like to see that bloke try it these days – Paddy is now the Police and Crime Commissioner for Nottinghamshire.

Chapter 5

PARTY CONFERENCES

Party conferences are brilliant and they're key events in the political year. Even after my first disastrously disappointing experience at the SWP conference, I viewed them as the holy grail of events. If I met someone who'd been to one, I'd ask them a million questions about it, as if they'd seen Oasis at Knebworth. I just thought they were massive gigs; I didn't appreciate what they actually involved.

What I got to find out is that party conferences are totally bonkers. If you've only ever seen them on telly, then you might think they're like conferences you've been to with work, where you spend day after day in a stifling room listening to boring speeches. And you'd be right about that. But there's also a whole load of other stuff that goes on which you don't see: like-minded activists from across the country coming together to share ideas and then hating each other over a week of fringe events, parties, lobbying events and keynote speeches.

It's tempting to compare these gatherings to music festivals, with a line-up of headliners and support acts, smaller stages and people being sick into bushes. But there are subtle differences, apart from the obvious, like festivals aren't defined by endless internal warfare and party conferences aren't easy places to get hold of MDMA (which has been a real shame for anyone going to the Labour conference in the last ten years). I've been to a few Labour, Conservative and Lib Dem conferences over the years so I can enlighten you on the madness and brilliance that you'll find there.

The first thing to know is that they're different for each party. The Labour Party conference is the sovereign decision-making body of the party. Every local Labour Party sends a delegate to vote a particular way on big policy decisions which take place on the conference floor. It is serious and highly contentious for this reason. Every autumn the deep divisions in the party are re-exposed during fraught votes, the outcome of which then become Labour Party policy.

I've always thought it's a daft way to make policy. Rather than allowing a leader the space to come up with their own ideas, Labour turns every issue into a referendum on their leadership. It creates a needless annual drama where the grassroots members are pandered to in a way that makes them look like they're the wisest people in the land. Spoiler alert: they're not.

The Conservatives don't do this. Their annual conference does not have any power. It's just a big get-together. Which means there are far fewer people there, it's less tense, but it's also less exciting. Anyway, what do they know? They've only been in power for ten years, increasing their vote share at all of the last four elections.

What they all have in common with Labour is the same basic structure: a main hall with keynote speeches and plenary sessions; an exhibition hall full of charities, businesses, campaign groups and others trying to entice visitors with sweets and games to raise awareness of their issues (sugar tax and the evils of gaming); fringe events that take place in different venues; and a load of bars and a load of parties.

You can choose what sort of week to have. You could have a stimulating week going to high-level policy discussions with experts from around the world and networking with like-minded folk from across the movement. You might want to spend most of your time in the main hall, watching frontbenchers and members speak from the podium. Or you can wake up every morning with a stinking hangover from being up in the hotel bar the night before, quickly shower while you remember you drunkenly called a junior minister a prick, wolf down a full English, have a couple of Alka-Seltzer with a Lucozade to steady the ship and dash to the conference centre to help prepare for the prime minister's speech. That's how I did it anyway.

When you're in government, conference feels big and important. The world's media are there, there's a heavy police presence, hordes of protestors beating at the door, and there is an ongoing intensity that comes from having the prime minister and cabinet all on site together. As a visitor, you're in the mix with all of them, ensconced in the same cocoon. Everywhere you look are the most powerful people in the country. For most of us that's not true the rest of the year.

When you're the opposition, the atmosphere is different. When you've just lost, these conferences feel flat. There is no magic. There are fewer protestors from your own camp for starters. Which sounds like a good thing, but when the bloke ranting about lizard people doesn't think you're worth bothering with, you know you're on the way to rock bottom. When you're fully in the wilderness it's like observing wildlife. I only went to one Labour conference under Corbyn. It was like going to an abandoned school that had been taken over by squatters. Now all the protestors who used to rant about lizard people were inside taking part. I expected to find sections of the building on fire.

The last Labour conference I attended was a far cry from my first Labour Party annual conference in 2006. I'd been to some smaller ones before then – spring conferences, youth conferences and regional conferences – but this was the first major one I'd been to and I was there as a member of staff. At the start I had that feeling you get on the first day of a holiday: I had the whole thing opening up before me and life was full of possibilities. Who knew what wonders the week would bring? I was in heaven. Well, Manchester, but to me that was the same thing. All of my favourite bands were from Manchester. The venue was the GMEX, which I'd first seen on a live Oasis video from their 'Be Here Now' tour. It was meant to be (here now).

We knew it was going to be a momentous event because Tony Blair had just announced that this would be his last conference as leader. It was going to be his farewell to the party. I didn't appreciate at the start of the week how emotional it was going to get and was more preoccupied with making sure I was up early to get the most out of the hotel breakfast. In case you're wondering, full English followed by a bowl of Coco Pops. Adding more and more Lucozade as my morning beverage each day.

Our first priority as regional staff was our delegates. In the run-up to the event we'd put on a few sessions in Nottingham so that those attending for the first time knew what to expect. It was also a way to find out what they were interested in so we could introduce them to relevant MPs and ministers once we got to Manchester. It was also a way to figure out who might be trouble. The Labour Party still had an anxiety around conferences, partly informed by the Militant experience of the 1980s. The last thing you wanted was for it to descend into heckling and protest, however legitimate you might find those things as part of a healthy democracy.

Before my time Labour conferences had been unruly. This might have been entertaining for the demagogues who revelled in conflict, but it repelled the public who rightly judged the party to be self-obsessed and immature. I borrowed a crowd control tactic off a colleague who'd used it in the past and swore it worked. If I thought one of our delegates was starting to prickle up or I could hear them begin to grumble, I wouldn't ask them to be quiet or to settle down because I knew that would just inflame them.

Instead, I'd tell them that the minister they wanted to see was ready to have a coffee with them right now. They'd leap up and follow me out of the hall while I frantically texted the minister to meet us at Starbucks. My colleague was right: it never failed. I was less Machiavelli, more Mochavelli.

In 2006 there were a load of parties or receptions every night. They were thrown by trade unions, lobby groups and broadcasters. Most were terrible and involved standing around in a hot hotel suite drinking acrid red wine while the M&S sandwiches began to curl on a platter in the corner. I'd still eat a few. Each Labour region had their own reception which the leader attended, as well as all the MPs and ministers from the area. Our room was too small. It started to get full very quickly – everyone was waiting for the leader. I knew Tony Blair was about to arrive because a load of new people we'd not invited swarmed into the already cramped room. These people follow the leader to every reception by finding out where they're going next and then running ahead. For what reason I don't know; maybe they like to hear the same jokes over and again. In which case they'd have loved my last tour. Tony and Cherie moved at pace, they swept in and if we didn't grab them and chaperone them, they'd be lost in the crowd. We had to get them to the microphone quickly so they could make a speech and then get them out. I was assigned to Cherie. It was like being security for a boxer on a ringwalk. I'd ask people politely to move back a bit, but they never did, so I'd have to just push through a crowd which was tightening around us like zombies hungry for brains. It wasn't the job for a claustrophobic. Some other events were even worse. Northern Night was a mega reception for the North East and North West and that was mayhem. The place was heaving. We had to link arms to form a human barrier so that Tony Blair could safely get in, as the drunk crowd surged forward, barging us all back. Some old northern bloke tried to push through me, his arms reaching over my shoulder to get near Blair. He was livid with me for getting in his way, looked me in the eye and went, 'Fucking hell, man, I just wanted to touch him,' as if Blair possessed healing properties.

The day of Blair's final speech to the party came and the atmosphere noticeably changed. Until that point the party hadn't confronted how it would feel to have their most dominant figure say goodbye. I thought the party felt confused. His supporters were sad and even his harshest critics in Labour had to accept he'd made the party more successful than any other leader in history.

I got to play a small part on that day, helping set up the 'departure shot' for his walk from the hotel to the conference centre. You know that totally normal sight, when a politician leaves a building and there's a group of people cheering in a pen? That. I hate to break it to you, but that moment is fully orchestrated: you would never get a perfectly diverse selection of the public passing by at that very instant and then spontaneously bursting into applause. It was my job to find twenty Labour members to applaud the leader of the Labour Party. Which sounds like an easy enough task, but it couldn't be any twenty people, it had to be balanced, because you can't just have twenty white blokes in suits behind a barrier or it'd look like the hospitality area at Twickenham.

I was rushing around the conference for hours trying to assemble the right mix of clappers. I felt like an *Apprentice* candidate panicking in Borough Market. 'I need two more old people, are there any old people?' I finally got my group together. I then waited inside the hotel entrance until I saw Tony and Cherie Blair come down the stairs, nipped outside ahead of them and started the applause as they emerged. That's right – for a brief moment I was basically the prime minister's right-hand man. I'm still slightly gutted he didn't thank me in the speech, to be honest.

Before Blair left office, there was one last gig – one final flourish – while he was still prime minister: on 10 May 2007, he would officially resign as prime minister and MP for Sedgefield at the Trimdon Labour Club. A few of us made it up to the North East for it, and we met for dinner the night before. As it now really was the end of an era, we had a few beers. While most people drifted off to bed, I stayed up at the bar with a friend of mine, a press officer called Iain Bundred. The next thing I knew we were doing Jägerbombs with a guy who was showing me bullet wounds on his torso. I remember that at one point, I knew this wasn't a normal situation, and felt a mild sense of peril: imagine something bad happened and the prime minister's resignation was overshadowed by a hostage situation involving two drunk members of party staff. But then again, Iain Bundred was way more sensible than me and he seemed fine with it. On reflection, he might have just been drunker than me. We carried on drinking, until the guy started telling us about the other times he'd been attacked by gunmen. At that point we decided to call it a night and only have a few more shots with him. Which felt an inappropriate thing to say given the cause of his wounds.

So, there I was the following day, watching Tony Blair as he said goodbye at the top of his game. Again. People who work in politics get the chance to be present at big moments in history. If you work for the Labour Party, those moments have been rare. I knew being in the room when a prime minister resigned was something very special. I also knew I shouldn't have had those Jägerbombs. The room was packed and it was red hot, so I tactically positioned myself near the door to get some breeze. I started to worry that I might be sick. I began to catastrophise, gripped by the horror that I might ruin a prime ministerial resignation by puking everywhere. On live TV. I'd be like one of those drunk yobs on shows like *Boozed Up Brits Abroad*. My career would be over and I'd bring shame on my family. I could see the news footage of my mum getting doorstepped and telling the cameras, 'He's only got himself to blame, I don't know why he drinks those horrible-sounding things, what are they called, Yemen bombs?' I'd have to leave my job; I'd never find work again. I pictured myself walking into job interviews and the person on the other side of the table going, 'Oh, you're the guy who puked during Tony Blair's resignation! I didn't recognise you without carrot chunks all down your front.'

I know it would make for a much better story had all this happened, so I hate to let you down. I managed to hold it together and wasn't sick. It's funny, though, whenever I see footage of that day, I have a Pavlovian response. My mouth goes dry and I start to feel too warm.

While the 2006 Labour conference was emotional, the following one in 2007 was intense. We were in Bournemouth for Gordon Brown's first Labour conference since he became prime minister. From the moment we arrived, the whole place was consumed by feverish rumours he was thinking of calling a snap election. He'd got off to a good start as prime minister and was outperforming David Cameron, who the public hadn't really figured out yet. Labour's poll ratings had lifted and despite private reservations that there was chaos behind the scenes in Downing Street, this welcome good news started to go to people's heads. Activists and politicians who'd become incrementally glummer over the last year or so had got their mojo back. It was like a collective mania had broken out.

I had a really ominous feeling about it. To me, it smacked of things getting out of control, like the discipline of the Blair years had evaporated. Gordon had repeatedly said there was no need for an election so I thought that would be problematic. I worried about party machinery as we didn't have anywhere near enough staff. Plus, some of the local parties in our marginal seats were deeply dysfunctional. Over the course of the week things became more bizarre.

One of my jobs was to lead the applause during the prime minister's speech. I was given an advance copy of the text and big 'X's marked the points at which they wanted the hall to applaud. There was an X after every paragraph. They basically wanted a round of applause for everything he said. I thought most people in the hall would have naturally applauded at some of these points but there were a few awkward times when I started on my own and had to keep going until everyone else – thousands of people – joined in. A couple of people kept looking round at me as I was noticeably clapping before everyone else and wouldn't stop until others had joined in. I must've looked like one of those toy monkeys that incessantly whack cymbals together. God knows why I wore the fez. I clapped so much my back ached. I can fully recommend it as exercise, I reckon I burned off about 700 calories during that hour.

It was a superb speech. All of Gordon's conference speeches as leader were excellent. I loved his booming, rumbling style that helped him convey a real sense of moral urgency. At that point he felt like a father of the nation. John Smeaton was sitting a few rows in front of me at that 2007 conference and got namechecked in the speech. He was the baggage handler who'd intervened to stop a terrorist attack at Glasgow airport by kicking one of the terrorists in the balls. It seemed like such a funny thing to be honouring. Obviously, Gordon framed it in diplomatic language but still, an arena full of people gave a standing ovation to a guy for kicking another guy in the nuts. Makes you proud to be British.

The election rumours were going mad. Personally, I didn't think there was any truth in them. Then I got called into a meeting with one of my bosses and a handful of other people. We were told that the election was on, that it was going to be in November and that we had to leave the conference now, go back to our offices immediately, get the printers going and have our candidates in marginal seats out campaigning that weekend. Well, holy shit. I couldn't believe it! I'd been let in on a huge secret, and it was one of the single most thrilling experiences of my life. It was the story that everyone was talking about and I had got privileged information about it. I felt dizzy walking through the conference centre knowing what was about to happen. I was also paranoid that people were going to see me and I'd somehow give the secret away with a facial expression: 'Look at him! He knows, he's been told there's going to be an election!'

I went back to my hotel, packed my case and began the 200-mile journey back to Nottingham. Except, that's not exactly what I did. I made one small diversion that could have got me into a lot of trouble.

Before I left, I had a nagging thought. I'd been handed a golden ticket. It was like being in a film where you find out the football results before they've happened. What is the first thing you'd think of doing in that scenario? Yes, that's right, I checked the Ladbrokes website. An election in the first two weeks of November was priced at 8/1. Free money. I didn't have much to bet with and I wasn't going to borrow money to gamble with, so I put fifty quid on. It would be the easiest £400 I'd ever make. About 1 per cent of me thought, *Just be careful, the election might not happen.* Luckily, I listened to that 1 per cent, otherwise I might have put £100 on.

The moment I'd paid I began to worry about whether I could get prosecuted for insider trading. All the way back to Nottingham I oscillated between imagining going to prison and wondering if I should have bet more. Either way, I was going to have an extra £400, so I also fantasised about how I would spend it. My dreams were modest: a haircut, a new pair of shoes and some pasties. Yes, you read that right. The limit of my ambition for my windfall was to go to Greggs. I didn't deserve the money.

The next day, back in the office, I was carrying a heavy box of paper into the office when I was told. My boss was on the phone and it sounded serious. She hung up and looked at me. 'It's off, he's not going to call the election.' I dropped the box on my foot. The pain was nothing compared to the emotional hurt I was feeling – my £400 pasty fund had just evaporated and I couldn't tell anyone about it. It was completely deflating. An election would have been stressful and hard, but it gives you a great purpose. I hadn't fought an election as a member of party staff and was keen to experience it. I wanted to be part of that huge collective effort and I wanted to be able to measure the success of the work I'd done by helping local parties hold those marginal seats.

It was also a PR disaster. In not calling the election, we looked scared. In that moment I thought that whenever the election came, we'd be toast. By the time the election came round in 2010 I wasn't working for the party anymore. The seats I'd helped all fell to the Tories: Corby, Northampton North, Broxtowe and Lincoln. History could have been very different had the election gone ahead in 2007. On the one hand, we may have won another term in office; on the other, I'd probably be a lot fatter after my £400 pasty banquet had spiralled into a full-scale habit.

The annual conference is the big one which gets all the attention, but there are other events peppered throughout the calendar. Things like the regional conference, the spring conference, the youth conference and the women's conference. The regional conference was always the most depressing. If the annual conference is Glastonbury, the regional conference is two blokes drinking in the park. That's not even an analogy, that's just what happens. The youth conference was always a nightmare. I never enjoyed it because I found most young members to be weird. They'd make really serious, earnest speeches about campus Labour clubs needing to 'share best practice' as if they were speaking about matters of war and peace. I thought most of them were pompous twerps swanning around pretending to be important. At least they were well prepared for a career in politics.

We had a youth conference at the Armadillo in Glasgow in 2007. Tony Blair was speaking so there were a lot of anti-war protestors and a heavy police presence. For whatever reason, I ended up being positioned near the front of the venue. The police were on high alert as they believed a number of protestors had managed to get into the event and were going to disrupt the speech. The fear of a terrorist getting in was always lingering, particularly after 7/7. Plonked near reception, I saw literally nothing of the event the whole weekend. Apart from one important thing.

The reception area emptied as everyone made their way into the auditorium. In the bar area I grabbed a seat and pretended to look busy while avoiding getting asked to do anything. Just as I did this, a shifty middle-class woman in reception answered her phone and said, 'Yeah, a few of us just walked in, they've got no idea. I'll unfurl the Palestinian flag and that's your signal.' Oh my God. This was too good to be true. I tried to make it look like I hadn't heard and got up as subtly as I could, popped outside and told the police chief what I'd heard. I say police chief – he was clearly in charge, but I don't know what rank he was. He had a very impressive hat with laurels on. He was also very serious. He had that hardness American generals have where it's almost handsomeness but not quite, because they're a bit too scary.

This guy was amazing. 'Right,' he said to a group of coppers, and they followed him. They then lined up side by side, forming two queues outside the entrance. Once I'd identified the pro-testors, they were individually ejected and brought in front of this Glasgow lawman. 'Do you know why you have been evicted from the event? You will now be transported to the designated protest area. If you leave the designated protest area, you may be arrested. Do you understand?' Any petulant mumbling meant the question was put again. 'Do you understand?' Once they made it clear that they understood, two coppers came forward and marched them to the designated protest area. Thanks to my intelligence gathering skills, a crisis had been averted. I felt like I was a member of Special Branch. Even if I had gathered the intel by skiving in the lobby.

But it was at my first Conservative Party conference later that year that my undercover skills were taken to the next level. I'd been seconded to the North West region to help on the 2007 local elec-tions. The Tories were having their Spring Forum in Manchester.

Security was light as they were in opposition and it wasn't their bigger annual conference. A few of us had chatted about it in the office and decided that a couple of us would just hang around in the bar and try and find out where David Cameron was going to be during the day so that we could ambush him with some Labour students and ruin his photos. We went to the Midland Hotel, where many party delegates were staying, headed for the bar and got chatting to some of the younger ones, including one young lad who asked us if we were going to the walkabout with Cameron the following day. He very kindly told us where and when it was going to be. I couldn't believe how easy it had been. We phoned it in and the next day, when David Cameron met the media in the street, a load of Labour students leapt out with banners and a huge pair of flip-flops with 'FLIP-FLOP' written across them, just in case you hadn't got the message. Emboldened by this, two of us decided to go back the following night and see what else we could find out.

The second mission was more brazen. We made a bit more effort, with fake names and a backstory just in case anyone asked us who we were. I chose a name I could remember well and took my dad's first name and my grandad's surname, which gave me the unremarkable combination of John Gleeson. Telling you this comes at a price: I've had to change all the security questions on my internet banking. My colleague Gregor Poynton took a different approach and just made one up. He went for Sam Bond, which sounded way better. I was a bit jealous.

I made us fake conference packs by printing off a load of conference documents the Tories had put on their website. It was something to stick in a folder and walk around with, in that way that delegates do. Sam and John had met in Nottingham and set up a PR firm. They were new to the party and were getting involved because they liked Cameron. It was a daft thing to do because if we'd had our cover blown, we would have been in massive trouble. Can you imagine the political fuss the Tories would rightly have made of it? Our careers would definitely have been over, we'd have been completely disowned by the party.

We returned to the Midland Hotel and headed straight back to the hotel bar. It was packed because in the suite just beyond the bar, David Cameron was hosting a leader's reception. We knew it was our mission to get into that reception. What followed was beyond our wildest dreams.

At this point we'd had a couple of drinks and were enjoying the sport of it more than pursuing any real political objective. It was such a rush; we were in the lion's den and the lions were all drinking champagne. We convinced ourselves we had to drink champagne to fit in. As we quaffed the stuff down, we saw the guests start filtering into the grand room where David Cameron was due to be. They were having their names checked off the list. Emboldened by the booze, we approached the table and gave two names which we knew would not be on the list because they were our very own inventions. OK, there was an outside chance someone called Sam Bond might have been on the list, but it wasn't highly likely. As for John Gleeson . . .

I knew from working similar events at the Labour conference that there are always a few people who aren't on the list. If they make a fuss, they'll often get let in just in case they might be powerful and also because you don't want to annoy them or look like you don't know who they are. I'm embarrassed to say that I used that knowledge to our advantage. When it was obvious our (made-up) names weren't on the list and so we couldn't come in, I got shirty. I put on my best posh accent. 'Oh, come on, this is getting ridiculous. I got the email about it, I got the text about it, I replied to them all. We know David, and this is just embarrassing. I don't want to have to make a complaint about this, but I might bloody have to.' I didn't want to go too far as I felt bad for the guy with the list. But then he asked us what region we were from and I told him we were from Conservative Future East Midlands. Instantly, he said 'Oh, are you with . . .' and mentioned a party official whose name I've now sadly forgotten. Let's say it was a normal Tory name like Quentin Harpoon. 'Are you with Quentin Harpoon?' he asked. It was an open goal. 'Harpy, I bet the old bastard's drunk half the red already,' I replied. With that, we were in.

Things got even more incredible.

Gregor and I positioned ourselves in the corner behind a big post. I was wary of the guy on the door bringing Quentin Harpoon over. I know this is obvious, but there were Tories everywhere: George Osborne, Francis Maude, Oliver Letwin . . . It was like the Road Dahl book *The Witches* – we were in their inner sanctum. I just hoped we didn't get turned into mice. The drink was flowing now, with trays of free fizz circulating, and I was pouring it down to try and calm my nerves a bit. Being sociable animals, we started mingling. Which was needlessly risky. Not as risky as what we did next. George Osborne was completely different to how I'd imagined him. He was very friendly and charming. The logical next step was to get a photo with him. We both had our photographs taken with him and Francis Maude. Then David Cameron walked in. It wasn't like the reception Tony Blair or Gordon Brown got at their conferences. It was a bit muted. Tories back then didn't go doolally over their leaders like Labour folk did, they were too posh.

It was odd seeing Cameron up close. He'd seemed a likeable bloke on telly and although I was Labour, I quite liked him. The next thing I knew I was shaking his hand and getting a photo with him too. What started as a bit of fun had escalated out of control. I couldn't wait to tell everyone at the office. This was off the chart. We'd blagged our way in and were now drinking with David Cameron. I was buzzing, I couldn't believe how audacious it was.

Our adventure wasn't over yet. In fact, it was about to become very perilous.

Gregor thought he'd spotted Christopher Hitchens. I didn't think the fella looked like Hitchens, but we were both giddy from drink and mischief so decided it was worth the risk of approaching him. He was chatting to a woman and we interrupted them to ask if he was indeed Christopher Hitchens. 'No, I'm Benedict Brogan from the *Daily Mail*.' That hit me like a mallet. We both immediately clammed up; this romp was now becoming dangerous. The journalist then introduced us to his friend. 'Oh, and don't talk to her, she's a mole.' I thought all my internal organs were going to collapse out of my arse. I sobered up instantly. They know. They're on to us and they're going to toy with us for sport. The joke's on us and this is how it ends.

'What do you mean, she's a mole?' I managed to say. The woman then revealed that she was a Tory but had been volunteering at Labour's head office and feeding intel back to CCHQ. I couldn't handle it. 'Bloody hell, old girl, you've got some gumption,' I replied, because that's how my brain thought all Tories spoke. I couldn't believe this. What a turnaround. Not only were we safe, we'd got some actual intelligence. There was just one problem.

I woke up the following day like Scrooge on Christmas morning. Life had so much joy! Gregor and I were sharing a house together and we couldn't wait to get to the office and tell everyone what had happened. Once there, we showed everyone the photos, regaling them with the minor details, stretching the story out for as long as we could. We revelled in every second of it. Then came the bonus – we'd found a mole. On top of everything, we'd actually been useful. Well, that would remain to be seen: we couldn't provide one crucial bit of information. We were both so fuddled, we couldn't remember her name. We couldn't even describe what she looked like. 'Er, well, like a woman. She had hair . . .' Amazingly, with what little we gave them, they were able to figure out who she was. Later that afternoon a call came from head office. They'd found her and kicked her out. They'd been wondering where certain leaks had been coming from and now they knew.

The absolute astounding irony of it! Two chancers go under-cover and they manage to expose someone else up to exactly the same thing. That was the highlight of my political career.

Once I'd moved on and had stopped working for the Labour Party, it felt strange going to the annual conference. I still loved going back and catching up with friends, but the atmosphere had changed. Each year I'd go, remembering how it had been in the Blair and Brown years and hoping it would have that buzz. It never did.

If only we'd known how much worse it was going to get. It was hard to be around the party when I believed it was so clearly heading in the wrong direction. It felt like the party was pretending to be serious rather than actually acting seriously. If they were serious, they wouldn't have chosen Ed Miliband as their leader. I know Jeremy Corbyn has created a new rock bottom since, but the Ed Miliband years were completely depressing. For all I respect Ed Miliband and his intelligence, trying to convince the country that someone is leadership material when they demonstrably aren't really devalues everything else you say. Labour wasted five toe-curling years selling Ed Miliband as a statesman. You'd have an easier job selling Cillit Bang as gin.

It was worse for friends of mine who had to stay and work for the party under a leader they knew would lose. I wasn't at the conference where Ed Miliband was unveiled as leader, but mates of mine on the staff were gutted. One of them got roaring drunk in one of the bars where Miliband's people were afterwards, held a pint aloft in each hand and shouted, 'We're fuuuucked, we're fuuuucked!' before being dragged out for the sake of his own career. It was a good job I hadn't been there because I'd have been doing the same thing. I'd have been on his shoulders, topless, tie round my head like Rambo before starting a small fire and dancing round it.

If I was at Brighton in 2013, I knew I wouldn't be able to stop myself murmuring during Miliband's leader's speech and didn't want to be a dick, so my mate Will Sherlock suggested watching it in one of the overflow rooms. Will is from a similar background to me. He's working class, from the East Midlands, more serious than me but with a really silly sense of humour. He'd been a special adviser and was working for Lexington Communications, an exceptional public relations firm. I'd never watched a speech in the overflow before so was up for a change that involved us being able to talk a bit, but mainly to take the piss. It turned out the overflow room was at the Brighton Odeon.

That's right: move over Bradley Cooper, Ed Miliband is coming soon to a cinema near you in *Limited*. I don't know if I've imagined this detail in retrospect but I'm sure I was so excited I bought one of those big bags of Maltesers in the foyer. As expected, the speech wasn't great, so we had a choice: we could either be depressed by it or we could find it funny. Put it this way, I haven't laughed in a cinema that much since I saw *Dumb and Dumber*. Not a word of it was taken seriously by us, as we slouched in our seats laughing so much we were squealing in physical pain. We were experiencing back-of-school-assembly levels of delirium. It began to catch on and others in the cinema started laughing along. As the speech wore on it became an unintentional comedy.

There are certain things you can never imagine yourself doing: infiltrating an illegal dog fighting ring; gun-running for a Mexican drug cartel; going to the Lib Dem conference. If you'd have asked me when I was working for Labour which one I was most likely to end up doing . . . well, I'd have said the Lib Dem conference one but it would still have been very unlikely. In 2016, I was there to do a light-hearted and slightly cheeky interview with their leader, Tim Farron, in front of an audience of Lib Dem politicians and activists.

The atmosphere took me by surprise. It is the politest political event I have ever been to. Anywhere. Scarred from years of Labour conferences riven by division, it was surreal to be at a (fairly large) gathering on the liberal left where people were happy. They smiled and everything. The Lib Dems had quickly come to terms with being obliterated at the 2015 election. I sensed that, like many Labour members, they were happier in opposition and relieved to be out of government. They also had that gentle Church of England vibe where even if you had said something appalling, they'd smile and clap anyway out of politeness. In an era when everyone is so sensitive about their opinion and apparently incapable of hearing criticism of their own side, what a wonderful novelty to be in a room laughing with people I'd campaigned against for years.

It was a small sign of hope that our politics would become more mature. Although, of course, being who I am, I couldn't help lowering the tone: one of my questions to Tim Farron was about a survey of sexual preferences among political activists which showed Lib Dems were more likely to be into bondage. He didn't deny it, but to be fair, his gimp mask was zipped up.

Chapter 6

TRICKS OF THE TRADE

I'm occasionally asked, 'What's the most important thing you've learned in politics?' That's easy – work in an office with good lunch options. Apart from that, here are some other lessons I learned, many through personal failure.

Lesson 1: Never repeat the charge

An old boss of mine used to say, 'If Candidate A puts out a leaflet saying that Candidate B is a paedophile, the last thing Candidate B should do is put out a leaflet saying, "I'm not a paedophile".' This is a great rule. Hopefully you'll never be accused of being a paedophile. Unless you are a paedophile, in which case I hope you are not just accused but apprehended.

For now, let's work on the assumption that you're not a paedophile.

I frequently had to calm down MPs who'd been wound up by an opponent's leaflet. Usually the Lib Dems'. They'd ring me up, going mad. 'It's full of lies! I need to put out a leaflet to correct the record.' Of course, if I was the candidate being insulted, I'd probably feel the same way, but it's the worst thing you can do. All you're doing is spreading the story. People won't remember where they heard it, or the details, so you're just creating more noise about whatever the allegation is. If they're calling you a dogger and you're then going door to door talking about how you're not a dogger, the only conversation you're having with people is about whether you're a dogger or not. And who goes into politics to do that? Don't answer that. Stick to your key messages, whether they're about the economy, the NHS or dog dirt, and keep pumping out materials that talk about that. Do not get involved in a tit-for-tat row where you're circulating rebuttal leaflets saying, 'My opponent has lied about me.' It devalues you. As my boss would say to other politicians, 'Don't get involved in a pissing contest.' A colleague of mine loved the story about Lyndon B. Johnson wanting to accuse an opponent of having sex with pigs. An adviser cautioned against it, telling Johnson that 'we can't get away with calling him a pig-fucker'. Johnson replied, 'I don't care, I want to hear him deny it.'

A slightly different version of this occurs in media interviews. Never repeat the charge in the question during your answer. If it's put to you that 'you have created a nation of bedwetters', do not let those words come out of your mouth. Think about how it sounds if you start your answer by saying, 'We haven't created a nation of bedwetters.' It sounds like you're accepting the premise of the question. You're helping reinforce an idea that because of your policies, people across Britain are now pissing the bed. Plus, when the interview is clipped for future use, the interviewer's question will be left out. It sounds like a framing that you chose, suggesting you're thinking about the issue in these terms.

Of course, not all questions are so obviously loaded, so you always have to be careful. The ploy might be more subtle, the accusation something gentle like, 'Why have you failed to miss your waiting-time target?' Don't repeat the f word. Take a moment to reset and say what you'd prepared to say. 'Under our party, the NHS sees more patients, carries out more operations and saves more lives than at any point in our history.' But only if it's true. Although that bit seems to be optional these days.

Lesson 2: Answer the question you want to answer, not the question you're asked

It's so easy to get blown off course in a media interview, and you may only be on air for a couple of minutes. If you treat the questions like a conversation, you'll be reactive and you won't be telling the public what you want them to hear. You'll come off air frustrated, wondering where the time went. Let's say you're doing an interview to promote your new policy of allowing teachers to taser problematic pupils. Not all pupils, you're not a monster. The interviewer might open by highlighting a weakness with it, something like, 'Amnesty International say that you're sick in the head and need psychiatric help.' The temptation is to react and have a conversation about how sick in the head you are. That would be a mistake. Stay focussed on getting your best lines out, regardless of the question. Something along these lines will do nicely:

'Parents and pupils watching this will know what a massive problem discipline has become in our schools. It's not fair that the kids who want to learn are held back by unruly and aggressive classmates, and it's not fair that teachers are intimidated while doing the most important job in society. All we're doing is giving teachers the basic powers they need to teach.'

(Incidentally, if you are ever on air defending that policy, please don't mention this book as an inspiration.)

This rule isn't without peril. You have to have a couple of clause sequences that don't make it sound like you're just repeating yourself word for word. If you keep repeating the same line over and over again, you can look disrespectful to the interviewer and by extension the public. Ed Miliband did this a few years ago, saying the exact same line for every question he was asked about an industrial dispute. No matter what was fired at him, he answered, 'These strikes are wrong, the government has acted in a provocative manner. I urge both sides to get around the negotiating table.' Ed, did you pay the water bill? 'These strikes are wrong, the government has acted in a provocative manner. I urge both sides to get around the negotiating table.' Hello, sir, can I take your drinks order and maybe get you some bread to start? 'These strikes are wrong, the government has acted in a provocative manner. I urge both sides to get around the negotiating table.'

To be fair to Ed Miliband, he also used a brilliant technique for sidestepping questions he didn't like. He'd listen to the question, ask himself a different question out loud and answer that one instead. It would go like this:

Interviewer: *Ed Miliband, do you think the public trust you with the economy?*
Ed Miliband: *If you're asking if I'll make the economy fairer, then the answer's yes.*

It happens so quickly you're dazzled by it. It's like having your pocket picked: it's only afterwards you realise what's happened. You almost have to respect the hustle.

Lesson 3: Don't become a reactive politician

This is particularly important for leaders and cabinet members, whether it's at national or local level. The system will swamp you if you're not careful. Your diary will get filled with a load of things, many of which you won't even understand the point of. You end up locked in the day-to-day of the job, being managed by it instead of taking charge of it. Then you wake up at election time and realise that you've put off all the things you wanted to do. It's not just about all the admin. If you're not disciplined, you end up being a reactive politician, bogged down in the same old arguments.

Think of ways to remove yourself from the daily political rows and speak directly to the public. I worked for the elected mayor of Stoke-on-Trent, Mark Meredith, during a tumultuous period where we were constantly firefighting against opponents inside and outside of the party. Every day was war. He had the brilliant idea of releasing Green Papers on various issues to set the agenda on things like the environment, which allowed him to have a dialogue directly with the public about a major issue. It meant that whatever the day-to-day battles were, he could remove himself from the fray and start a different conversation with the voters about issues they cared about. It's more satisfying, because it's what you came into politics for and it means you're defining yourself on your terms.

You have to keep campaigning when you're in office. If you're a council leader, schedule regular community meetings across your territory that give you direct contact with the public. Put your name on it and make a fuss about it being new. Call it something like Chris Cream's Community Forum. But only if your name is Chris Cream. I can't tell you what a huge mistake it would be if your name isn't Chris Cream. It will confuse the public, deprive you of the publicity and lead to questions about your state of mind. The first question at every event will be, 'Who is Chris Cream and why have you named a community forum after him? I don't understand it. No one understands it.'

Lesson 4: Journalists are lazy

A more sympathetic view might be that journalists are very busy. Either way, a journalist's way of doing their job is a gift for politicians. Get into the habit of writing press releases as if they're newspaper articles because when you send them in to the local paper, they'll often just publish them word for word. It's like magic. If you're really good, you can even get your own headline in there too. Even if they tinker with it a bit, it won't be a major departure from what you wrote. Insert quotes from you as if you've actually been interviewed. Something like:

Welcoming the new emphasis on school discipline, Priti said, 'They'll be a great addition to the school experience. Just like I was able to reminisce about getting the cane at school, the kids of the future will be able to reminisce about the time they got tasered.'

Think of it as a good deed. Lots of newspapers are understaffed. You're helping save them the bother of having to write another article. You've helpfully done it for them. Good on you.

Lesson 5: Saying 'this is off the record' doesn't make it off the record

I guarantee that right now there's a politician somewhere in the world forgetting this undisputed fact and destroying their career. Never say anything to a journalist that you wouldn't want to read or hear back in the media. I know. It's obvious. It's as obvious as saying, 'Never take your clothes off in public unless you want to be called a flasher.' Which is the story the journalist might be ringing up about. Journalists might be lazy (see lesson 4) but they're also wily. They don't sound how you expect them to sound. They'll call you up and sound chummy, even gentle and sympathetic. They know how to get you talking. If that doesn't work, they'll put words in your mouth. 'I know some MPs who think the prime minister interferes with dogs,' they might say. Don't even cough in response. Certainly don't get worn down into uttering the killer phrase, 'OK, but this is strictly off the record,' unless you want to see the headline *WHAT A HOUND: POOCH PERV PM'S PET PECCADILLO.*

The same goes for the phrase 'Chatham House rules'. If you're not familiar with the saying, it means what you're about to say cannot be repeated. It's basically a posh version of 'What happens in Vegas, stays in Vegas.' Telling a group of strangers that 'it's Chatham House rules' and then spilling the beans is one of the worst ways to keep a secret. Not only have you spread the story, you've also used the phrase 'Chatham House rules', which has made the story way more exciting and therefore way more spreadable.

Lesson 6: Tailor your message to your audience

This is so obvious it shouldn't need spelling out. In fact, I wouldn't have included it had I not met Dominic Raab. During the 2019 Conservative leadership election, I was invited to host a hustings for the One Nation group of Conservative MPs. This was at the height of the Brexit debate. I was to grill Michael Gove, Matt Hancock, Dominic Raab and Jeremy Hunt individually for half an hour each in a private parliamentary meeting of Conservative MPs. For a boy who grew up on benefits and had spent a political career opposing the Tory Party, it was quite a moment to be part of the process to pick the next Conservative prime minister. Part of me did wonder if I was betraying my entire upbringing, or if I was about to be ceremonially sacrificed. I was too intrigued to say no.

It was surreal to be the only person in the room who wasn't a Conservative MP. The hustings took place in the Grey Room in Parliament, a grand oak-panelled committee room with high ceilings and chandeliers. From my view at the top table, I looked down the middle of the room with two sides of benches facing each other, like a mini House of Commons. On my right were Churchill's grandson, Nicholas Soames, and the former Home Secretary, Amber Rudd. On my left was an empty chair that each candidate in turn would sit in during their half-hour slot. They were to wait outside the door in the corridor until they were called in for their turn. I had one last check that I wasn't naked so that I definitely knew I wasn't dreaming, and we began.

The One Nation group is the socially liberal and broadly pro-European wing of the Conservatives. Dominic Raab is hardly a natural ally of theirs so, to be fair to him, he was at a disadvantage on the night. That said, Michael Gove had been a far more prominent Leaver and had performed well at the beginning of the evening, tailoring his message to display his liberal values. Remember, at this stage we were still in a hung Parliament and still in the EU. The big fear was leaving on the then deadline of 31 October without a deal. Gove said he was prepared to extend the deadline for the UK leaving the EU beyond 31 October. This was important: he'd shown he was open to reason and didn't necessarily want to leave without a deal. Dominic Raab took a different approach. He wouldn't rule out proroguing Parliament, he wouldn't rule out a 'No Deal' Brexit and he wouldn't even rule out the involvement of Nigel Farage in negotiating a deal with the EU. Maybe that's perfectly legitimate if he thought a No Deal Brexit or the presence of Nigel Farage around the negotiating table are desirable things. Sadly, both things were completely batshit.

That wasn't really the problem. The problem was Raab's language and tone. He treated the event like it was a rerun of the 2016 referendum campaign and started delivering Vote Leave slogans to a room full of Remainers. He was dying on his arse. I had a quick scan round. He'd completely lost the room. I don't have any tattoos but if I was forced to have one, and I couldn't have a Nottingham Forest one, I'd have the expression on Philip Hammond's face tattooed on my arm. It's one of the funniest things I've ever seen. Simultaneously surprised and pitiful. Like a parent who's caught their son wanking.

In those moments when Raab was alienating his listeners I found it oddly levelling. Here I was in the bowels of Parliament, cross-examining candidates, one of whom could be the next prime minister, in a room of people who would help make that decision. The stakes could not have been higher. Yet even at this level, a leading politician was making basic mistakes that even council candidates would avoid. I thought back to all the candidate training exercises I'd done, to all the selection meetings I'd been to, and I was struggling to think of a candidate tanking so badly.

In the end Boris Johnson won, prorogued Parliament and did a deal with Nigel Farage during the general election which helped deliver him an eighty-seat majority. The One Nation group had been absolutely right to be suspicious.

Lesson 7: Know the rules of the contest

This is so basic, so simple, that it's degrading to all of us that I have to include it, but I've encountered politicians in all parties who'll be in a selection contest and not know the rules of it. I'm rubbing my eyes with frustration as these memories of almost heroic density come back to me.

Let's start with a standard parliamentary selection process. Say you want to be the Labour candidate for Sherwood when the selection process opens. Firstly, find out how to make the shortlist. If it's an all-women shortlist and you're a chap, then look elsewhere. Or consider surgery. Once you've cleared that hurdle, figure out how many nominations you need from local branches. Find out how many local branches there are. Who are the branch secretaries and chairs? How can you contact them and how soon? What about affiliate branches, through the trade unions and the Fabian Society, etc.?

Let's presume you make the shortlist. You then need to know when the deadline is, how many members you need to support you and how soon you can get their contact details so that you can canvass them. Ideally, you'd visit them all or ring each one of them personally. Make sure your supporters can make the selection meeting. See if they can convince their friends in the party to vote for you too. Not knowing the rules of a selection process is bad enough. Not knowing the rules of a major party's leadership contest that you're standing in is insane.

Yet there I found myself, at an unspecified location, sometime in the last couple of years casually chatting away to someone standing to be leader of their party. (I really don't want to give away who it is, because I don't want to hurt his feelings. Or her feelings.) I asked them if they knew when the deadline was for new members to join who could vote in the contest. This should not have been a bolt from the blue, but I am sorry to tell you that it absolutely was. At first it was like I'd suggested robbing a bank – they couldn't believe what I was saying. I decided to elaborate in case I'd perhaps worded the original question badly. 'If new members can still join and vote in the contest, you could recruit loads of new members who will then vote for you, like Jeremy Corbyn did.' I'd just been making small talk; I couldn't believe they didn't know one of the most important rules of the race. Especially in the context of a leadership contest taking place after Corbyn's initial leadership victory.

They took out their phone to message an adviser. I was tempted to ask them if they knew how to log in to the WiFi, but I thought they'd had enough revelations for one day and I didn't have the energy to explain what the internet was.

Lesson 8: Go into a meeting knowing what's going to happen

This is especially true of selection meetings. If you've got enough supporters to win and they're all there on the night, providing you don't say something stupid to alienate them, you'll win. Candidates who turn up on the night and wing it don't do very well. This is politics, not *Britain's Got Talent*. It's also true of general political meetings. Know what the aim of the meeting is and prepare for it. Make sure you have allies in the room and discuss with them in advance the things that each of you should say. Ask friendlier attendees if they'd be willing to speak in favour of your position once it's opened up to discussion (insider tip: trade unions are really good at this; they always turn up in numbers and they're well rehearsed).

This may sound like you're undermining the point of a meeting and effectively turning it into a choreographed play, where everyone else becomes unwitting spectators. But what is the point of a meeting? Surely it's to make decisions that lead to action? If you care about achieving a particular aim, why leave it to chance? If you're taking politics seriously, then breaking things down into these practical tasks becomes habit-forming and you become more adept at campaigning, organising and – hopefully – winning.

In the real world, this can be very hard to achieve. Trying to get your friends to come to a meeting about wheelie bins in a freezing community hall on a January night is hard enough, even if they don't have a family or any fun in their lives. Don't forget you can always resort to emotional blackmail and, failing that, actual blackmail.

Lesson 9: If you want an audience at your party conference fringe event, provide free booze

You'd love to think that the 500 politicos are queuing round the block because they're passionate about procurement solutions. In fact, they're there for the wine. Party conferences are less a festival of ideas and more a festival full stop. People go to wander around different stages, drink all day and try to have a transcendental mind-bending experience. Like hearing Richard Burgon speak. If your listing in the official guide mentions that there's free food and drink, you're guaranteed an audience. Delegates will be drawn from all over the site like ravers to bad music.

The opposite is also true. No booze, no people. Do you seriously expect anyone to come and sit in a sterile hotel suite for an hour while listening to a panel of bores drone on about the importance of 'reskilling' without a drink? It's the least you can provide them with. Think of it as a liquid apology: 'I'm so sorry you've chosen our event, here's a magnum of red to numb the pain.'

Lesson 10: Only stand for election if you want to get elected

Usually candidates are upset if they lose, but there's a select group of politicians out there who are gutted if they win. I realise this sounds ludicrous, so let me explain.

In certain parts of the country different parties will struggle to stand candidates in every seat at local elections. What's the point in contesting a seat you always lose by miles? Well, if you're a major party, you want to give everyone the opportunity to vote for you in every election because even if that particular council seat is impossible to win, it might be part of a winnable constituency and those voters could make all the difference at a general election. Plus, it's embarrassing if major parties can't find candidates.

So, you talk some friendly local activists into being 'paper' candidates. Their name goes on the ballot but they're not under any pressure to campaign there, it just allows people to vote Labour in as small a number as they wish.

There's just one flaw in this plan. The public doesn't always behave.

I was used to counselling distraught candidates who had lost. I never thought I'd have to counsel someone who'd won, but that's exactly what happened. Against our predictions one year, Labour had won a load of seats on the council that we hadn't expected to. The morning after this amazing success, I answered the office phone to a very angry person who shouted at me, 'You told me I wouldn't get elected!' I didn't know what to do, so I just started apologising. At first, I wasn't sure if it was a wind-up but it wasn't – he was genuinely annoyed. 'You told me there was no chance of me getting elected, now I've got to spend five years on the bloody council!' When he put it like that, I did start to feel sympathetic. If you weren't planning on it, having to take on the responsibility of being a publicly accountable politician all of a sudden is a bit of a drag. Add to that the tedium of council meetings and, well, I'm amazed he didn't have me killed.

Lesson 11: Voting against your own policy is a very bad idea

This isn't about backbench rebellions. This is about being a cabinet member and voting against a policy you still agree with. I know this must feel like a riddle, but there's no catch. I sat in a meeting where this was suggested. I won't say where or when this took place or what the issue was, because I really liked the person, but it was in a local authority and to my dismay, instead of immediately dismissing the idea, some of their colleagues agreed.

Some context is important. Not every politician is resilient. Criticism hurts. When it's sustained it can become unbearable.

Being a local politician is often a very hard job. There's none of the glamour of Westminster. You don't feel important at all, yet you experience all the downsides of responsibility. You can become a hate figure just for taking decisions in imperfect circumstances that aren't of your making. You're in a small place and it feels claustrophobic. The media attack you, which keeps the public inflamed. This isn't what public service was meant to feel like, so the temptation to find a way out becomes overwhelming. I understand all that, but the answer isn't to do something stupid which then alienates those still supporting you and makes you look like an idiot.

The policy in question was a good idea. In fact, it was a really good idea. The politicians in the discussion thought it was a really good idea. They'd come up with it and they still agreed with it. As with any change, some residents weren't happy, and it had become highly pressurised over a period of months. Some of the politicians were wobbling. I ended up in a meeting with them and that's when it happened. I was in the room when one of the worst suggestions in the history of politics was made. 'When it comes to the vote, we could propose the policy and then vote against it.'

It took a couple of seconds for it to sink in. I couldn't hear laughter. Where was the laughter? If someone didn't laugh, it was in danger of being taken seriously. Surely one of them was going to laugh? No one laughed. They were all so desperate to end the pain, they were taking it completely seriously, mulling it over like it was an unexpected bid to buy their car.

Incredibly some of them ended up doing it: proposing it and then voting against it. One even described it as a 'silver bullet'. I resisted telling them that the preciousness of the bullet is irrelevant if you're about to fire it into your own head.

Lesson 12: Never let a visit go ahead without a 'recce'

Visits. Simultaneously the most satisfying and terrifying experiences of a campaign. They provide the opportunity to get great footage of your candidate showing the prime minister around a new school surrounded by beaming faces, weighed against the clammy fear that someone is going to get egged.

I loved working on visits, despite having a total and utter nightmare on one very early in my career. It's great being able to take a minister to somewhere in a key battleground and have them chatting to the public. In my experience, the public love it, even if they're not really sure who the minister is or what they do. Someone from the government is in their local café or park and they get to tell them to their face what they think all the problems in the world are. It's direct politics.

A visit itself may only be an hour in a community hall but you have to think about absolutely everything that can go wrong. It's not just the obvious political problems – a protestor or a heckler – it's the basics, like how to get into and out of the building. I'll tell you about the time I completely cocked it up as an example of how overlooking a couple of small details can ruin everything.

It was during my time as a regional organiser. I was covering Northamptonshire and a council by-election had been triggered in Northampton. During the campaign we were offered a visit by Jim Knight, who was an education minister. Labour's big message at the time was the 'Respect' agenda. Tony Blair had been pictured removing some graffiti with a high-pressure hose in Swindon. Our press officer, an exceptional talent called Phil Dilks, suggested doing graffiti removal with Jim Knight. Perfect. They'd seen the prime minister doing it on the news, now they'd see their local Labour council candidate doing it with a government minister.

Firstly, I had to find somewhere in the ward covered in graffiti. It wasn't hard. In a small local square, a wall was plastered in it. Not arty stuff, just a load of words. That should have been my first concern. What would they remove the graffiti with, though? None of us had access to the high-pressure kit Tony Blair had used. Dilksy suggested using a mop and bucket. Old school. Fine. It would be a bit harder, but the message was the same. At the back of my mind I did wonder if it would actually work. Would a mop, bucket and a bit of bleach actually get this stuff off? Did that matter? It was just a quick stunt and the photo would still look good and get the message out – Labour politicians rolling up their sleeves to remove graffiti. Before I tell you what unfolded, think about what could go wrong. Guess what you think I overlooked. Got a theory? Good. Here we go.

Water. I hadn't thought about where we'd get water from. Why would I? Water is everywhere. Except it's not, is it? If you're using a mop and bucket at home, you just fill it up from your tap, but if you're driving someone else's mop and bucket to an estate in Northampton, where would you fill it up and what with? This is such a simple problem it hadn't occurred to me at all.

So here I was driving the candidate and the minister to the square with a mop, bucket and some Ajax in the boot. I knew something wasn't right, I could feel I'd overlooked something, and my brain was teasing me – dangling a nagging doubt but not giving me any details. I kept walking through the stunt in my mind and then it hit me. Where was I going to get water from? They don't just have taps in the street. I panicked and pulled into the first shop I saw. It was a Waitrose. It was the first time I'd ever been in one, and I'd heard they were pricey. I legged it to the bottled water and bought the cheapest ones I could find. Evian was on offer, so I bought a couple of large bottles. Phew, good save. Crisis averted. I can't be sure, but I think I might have even chuckled to myself about how awful it would have been had I realised the problem on arrival. We pulled up short of the square and I filled up the rusty, smelly bucket with France's finest mineral water, and tipped in a load of Ajax powder.

Some stereotypical local journalists were waiting for us. Not the modern sort, on their way to a bigger job at a national newspaper, but the dusty, cynical sort who struggle to return eye contact. They were there in the hope it would all go wrong, like the older boys who watch the school play so they can take the piss out of it. They could smell a mistake in the air.

Regardless, we walked over to the graffiti with the mop and bucket and that's when it dawned on me. The graffiti was pure filth. It was a wall covered in spurious gossip about other residents, accompanied in some cases by a mobile phone number. I saw 'Mick Sucks Dick' written in big letters and positioned myself in front of it so that it wasn't in any of the photos. Another fine save. Well played.

Jim and the candidate scrubbed away at the graffiti with the pathetic mop covered in Ajax and, unbeknown to anyone else there, French mineral water. A government minister was trying to remove lurid graffiti with Evian, but no one else knew so that bit was fine. When I got back to the office, I regaled my colleagues with the story.

The paper had got their photos and a story and the pair did a radio interview. They didn't manage to actually remove any graffiti, but they scrubbed hard and the photos would be great. I couldn't wait to read the piece with my feet on the desk while marvelling at my improvisational political genius. I'd have to get a copy sent to the office from someone in Northampton, but I could wait a few days.

As it happened, I didn't need to wait because when I arrived at work the following morning, someone had already faxed the article to the office.

The paper had a photo of me filling up the bucket with Evian and they'd printed it under the headline: *EAU YES HE DID*. The whole article was all about Labour being so out of touch they tried to clean up graffiti with mineral water. I was named in it. It was a total disaster. I'd heard of colleagues becoming a story before and it sounded awful, but that was usually for things a bit more political than being caught filling a bucket with Evian.

I was angry with myself for not being more careful when I'd filled it up. I hated the journalist who'd turned up to sneer and I was embarrassed I'd gifted him something to drool over. I felt sick. I was going hot, cold and then hot again. I was convinced I was going to get fired. The stakes felt so high. I'd not just wasted a minister's time and made them look idiotic, I'd harmed Labour's chance of winning that by-election and, by extension, I'd let down the Labour Party. My gaffe had helped damage the bloody government. Well, that's how it felt.

I didn't get fired, and my colleagues found it funny. Which was a relief, but I'd learned the importance of knowing every detail of a visit before it happens. I've not bought a bottle of Evian since, for drinking or cleaning. I do remember being relieved for one small detail. Thank God they didn't know I'd bought it from Waitrose.

Lesson 13: Brand yourself

The Phil Dilks I mentioned earlier was Labour's head of regional press. A former journalist, he knew how to give the media great content, especially great photos. He's one of the most brilliant, eccentric and charismatic colleagues I had working for the party. He had a great creative approach to politics and had managed to take a safe seat off the Tories on his local council despite being a

Labour Party member of staff. That's how good he was. He'd done it in the most audacious way and only he could have pulled it off.

As well as being predictably called 'Dilksy', he was also known locally as 'Fair Deal Phil'. Firstly, that is a great nickname for anyone. Secondly, most politicians wouldn't be able to believe their luck if they started getting called that. He might as well have been called 'Absolute Legend Phil'. He'd run a campaign around a 'fair deal' for bus passengers and had succeeded in overturning the council's decision about bus tokens. The local paper started calling him Fair Deal Phil, but it was a nickname he'd effectively given to himself that the media were now repeating (see lesson 4).

The more they used it, the more it became a reality. I stayed at his house a few years ago and we went for a curry. Everyone there knew him as Fair Deal Phil too. 'It's Fair Deal Phil!' a bloke shouted across to our table. Someone else joined in: 'How you doing, Fair Deal?' He'd created his own brand. That's impressive enough on its own but it also explains his stunning election and subsequent re-elections. The rules are more relaxed now, but back then, you had to appear on the ballot paper under your full real name yourself unless you could produce documentary evidence that you were known by another name. Barely anyone ever could, but Phil had reams of paper cuttings calling him Fair Deal Phil. He convinced the returning officer so that year, when every other candidate was listed as Surname, Firstname, Dilksy was on the ballot paper as Fair Deal Phil.

Lesson 14: Don't rely on the public to do the obvious thing

Brexit and Trump proved this on a grand scale, but the public have a proud history of not doing the obvious thing at election time.

A couple of years before I started working in Stoke, a councillor there was found guilty of incitement to distribute child pornography and placed on the sex offender's register. That was his political career over then? Nope. He was able to stay on as a councillor because he didn't get a custodial sentence so didn't miss any Full Council meetings. That in itself sends a toxic message: missing council meetings is worse than being a sex offender.

Surely once election time came around, he stood down to spare himself the blushes of being defeated? No, he stood again. Ah, but the voters must have been queuing round the block to vote him out? I don't know how to break this to you, but he got re-elected. In fact, he's still a councillor today fifteen years after his conviction. He's been re-elected multiple times. Maybe Candidate A put out a leaflet calling themselves a paedophile.

Lesson 15: You don't have to mark an 'X' on your ballot paper for your vote to be counted

Millions of us still believe that if you don't vote with an 'X' then your vote won't count. This is not true. The Electoral Commission guidelines are that, if in doubt, the returning officer 'should ask whether the voter has, on the face of the paper, indicated a reasonably clear intention to vote for a candidate'.* The word 'reasonably' is doing a lot of the work in that sentence. At every election count the spoiled ballots are shown to the candidate and agent of each party for them to agree that they're spoiled or to make the case that it represents a 'reasonably clear intention' to vote for them. This means all sorts of daubings could be considered as serious votes. If the count is close and there only one or two votes in it, the result can hang on whether a couple of spoiled ballots could be argued to be reasonably clear intentions of support.

We had a training session on it ahead of a big round of local elections, and I could not believe some of the stuff that's allowed.

The easiest one is a tick, only in the box of one candidate. That's clearly a vote. The Electoral Commission show on their website that they'll accept a smiley face drawn in the box of just one candidate as a vote. A cross or tick or a smiley face not in the box but just next to the name of a candidate would count too. Writing 'YES' in one box would count as a vote. What if they've written things in different boxes? Now it gets trickier. If they've written 'NO' in every other box but 'YES' in one, that would count as a vote for that candidate.

This is Britain, though, and some of our fellow citizens are so enthused by democracy, they're overcome with a desire to

---

* A footnote with a reference! This really is a proper book. The quote is from the Electoral Commission guidelines which you can find here: https://www.electoralcommission.org.uk/sites/default/files/pdf_file/UKPE-doubtfuls-booklet.pdf

broaden their vocabulary. In the 2019 European elections a voter in Leicester wrote 'WANK' next to every candidate, but 'NOT WANK' next to the Greens. It was counted as a vote. I was at a city count a few years ago where the whole council was up for election. We were in a leisure centre with about sixty different counts all going on at the same time. It was like being on a trading floor, it was chaos. I was there to help support our candidates in assessing spoiled ballots. Once you make the case that a tenuous one should go your way, you have to be prepared for the next one to be similarly tenuous the other way. I was stressed out so was trying to make the case for any spoiled ballot that I could to count as a Labour vote. That's how I ended up trying to convince a returning officer that although the voter had drawn a cock and balls on their ballot paper, the jet coming out of the end of it was landing in the Labour box. I didn't win that one.

So, if you're going to spoil your ballot, be careful about what you do as it might end up getting counted as a vote. I used to think it was odd that we didn't tell more people that any indication of support counts but that would make it even more chaotic than it is. Plus, you can't have it on party political broadcasts. 'I'm Keir Starmer. If you value the NHS, make sure you vote for it this Thursday by writing "WANK" next to everyone else's name, but "NOT WANK" next to the name of your local Labour candidate. Polls open at 7 a.m.'.

Lesson 16: If you're behind, ask for a recount. If you're ahead, don't

There's something about the atmosphere at an election count. It's late, everyone is tired and there's nothing you can do about the result. Which isn't strictly true. Parties watch every box closely, trying to get a sense of the result when they're first tipped onto the table and placed face down. Once the counting starts, you're watching every bit of paper, making sure that they're being put into the correct bundles. Mistakes can be made, where a bundle of Labour votes has a Conservative vote placed on top and then the whole pile wrongly gets counted as all Conservative votes.

Once the votes are counted and the returning officer tells the candidates and agents the result, if you're behind by a reasonable margin of error you've got to ask for a recount. The problem is at that stage of the night, sometimes two or three in the morning, you feel impolite for asking. The staff are exhausted and you're going to put them and you through it all over again. You've got to try it. If the result is pretty much the same, then maybe accept it, but if it narrows in your favour, ask again.

Always take a beat and think before you ask for a recount, though. After a recent election one candidate told me that when the result was announced it was close, so they shouted 'recount' before realising they were actually ahead.

Lesson 17: Never lose your shit in public

This is just a good rule for life. Never have a tantrum in the street, never have an argument in a supermarket. It's bad enough to see your neighbour do it, but once you've seen a politician have a tantrum in public, it's impossible to fully respect them again. It's a rare sight but it usually happens during a by-election. The relentless hours of campaigning every day, the whole party machinery decamping to their area and the national focus just on them takes its toll and they can develop what colleagues used to call 'candidate-itis'. Inflammation of the candidate. Which sounds like a euphemism. They go mad. They feel like they're not in control of the campaign and that they're not being listened to. (N.B. they're not necessarily wrong.)

Eventually they snap, usually over something trivial. When it happens, it's shocking. A grown adult has lost all reason and now they're screaming and stamping their feet. In a street they're about to canvass for votes. It's also hilarious but you cannot laugh because that makes things worse. You have to treat them as you would a child: talk in a calming voice and try to lower the intensity of the situation by agreeing with them and soothing them.

I saw a great strop during a parliamentary by-election. Things had been getting increasingly strained with the candidate and we were in the final fortnight of the campaign. A colleague and I were meeting him on an estate with a boot full of leaflets. I knew we were in trouble because even though we were early, his first words to us were 'you're late'. We were the outsiders; he was standing with a circle of local activists and I got the impression he'd been chuntering away about us before we arrived.

We ignored the slight and handed out bundles of leaflets to everyone to shove through the door if people didn't answer or to hand to them if they were in. The candidate asked to see the leaflet, so I handed him one and he screwed his face up at it like I'd handed him a dead pigeon. 'We're not delivering these.' Uh-oh, here we go. I manage to choke out a reply: 'Er, but . . . what else will we deliver?' He didn't care. 'I don't know, go back and get something else, but we're not putting these through people's doors.' There was nothing wrong with the leaflets, he just wanted to have a go at us.

The other member of party staff said, 'Well, the rest of us will deliver them then.' That was the point of no return. The candidate must have had a couple of hundred leaflets in his hand. He paused and then slung them into the air, like people who've just won a million dollars do on films. As the leaflets rained down like propaganda confetti, he kicked a wall. I had to turn away so that I didn't burst out laughing. I was at back-of-class levels of laughter suppression. He walked off leaving us to pick up his litter. I'd heard of tidying up a politician's mess, but I never thought I'd have to do it so literally.

Chapter 7

EARLY WARNING SIGNS

On the evening of 23 June 2016, I was at the Royal Festival Hall to celebrate what I confidently thought would be a Remain victory in the EU Referendum. I was delighted to be invited to the venue where Labour had partied the night of that first election victory in 1997. The atmosphere was very New Labour. It felt bright and upbeat; moderate politicians from all parties were mingling and drinking together. For the first time in years I was at a political gathering that made me feel positive. Despite the horrendous behaviour of some politicians during the campaign, standing in that room gave me real hope for the future.

That feeling lasted about an hour, and then the first result came in. Sunderland had voted to leave by a margin of 61 per cent to 39 per cent, far bigger than expected. From that point onwards, the night never recovered. As the hours ticked by, the horror slowly unfolded like a nappy full of shit. Once it was beyond doubt, I found myself on the balcony just staring forlornly across the river at Big Ben (yes, I know it's the name of the bell, but you know what I mean) as if it was going to give me an explanation. Or fall down. I don't know what I expected but I couldn't stop staring at it. Part of me wanted to cry so that I could enjoy the little lift you get afterwards, but I wasn't upset in that way. I just couldn't process it. It was like turning up to see your team get presented with the Premier League trophy only to find out that the presentation had been cancelled and, by the way, you've been relegated. Or to use a more contemporary example, think that Forest are going to make the play-offs only for them to drop out of them in the final five minutes of the season on fucking goal difference. Sorry, it's still raw.

I had the ominous feeling that I didn't know my own country anymore. I'd experienced plenty of political defeats in the past, but I had always been able to rationalise them. This one had taken me by surprise. But it shouldn't have done. There'd been so many warning signs in the years leading up to that referendum, and plenty during the campaign, but I'd never appreciated how serious they were.

The first proper indication to me that mainstream politics was under threat was during my time working in Stoke. When I arrived in 2007, the BNP had nine out of sixty seats on the council. NINE. In 2007. This wasn't the 1980s of *This is England*. This was 2007. There were iPhones in 2007. Facebook was part of normal life. José Mourinho was managing in the Premier League. It's not a long time ago. Labour were in government. OK, now you mention it, that does feel like quite a long time ago.

I'd ended up in Stoke for a couple of reasons. Firstly, working for Labour directly had become impossible. The party had huge debts and regional staff had been completely stripped out. I didn't feel like I had any job security. Harold Wilson House, an office that ideally would have had ten or more staff, now had just three. There were only three of us to manage a vast area, full of precarious marginal seats. No matter how hard we worked, no matter how many hours we put in, there was no way we could do a decent job. Politics is always chaotic, consuming and demanding. You expect your phone to ring all hours of the day and night, but I never minded that bit. It was the total lack of resources that drove me mad. Every MP and every local party expected the same level of service. Very few were understanding about the pressures we were under.

The hours became punishing rather than exhilarating. As a party we were proud about bringing in the Working Time Directive which meant staff couldn't be forced to work more than forty-eight hours a week. What we never said was that this didn't apply to Labour staff. I was regularly working seventy- and eighty-hour weeks. Probably more. The party of the workers was running its own workers ragged. Trousered philanthropists they weren't.

I'd recently met Mark Meredith. He was one of a new, rare breed of elected mayors and had been elected to run Stoke-on-Trent at just thirty-nine years old. He was highly impressive and as well as spending a life in the Labour Party had successfully run his own business. Mark was the sort of politician I liked – an optimist to his core. He was endlessly positive, full of energy and was impatient to get big things done for Stoke, a place rapidly falling behind the rest of the country. He was looking for a political adviser and I fancied a new challenge. I'd been warned that the politics in Stoke was, as a colleague put it, 'fucked'. I wondered how bad it could really be given what I'd already experienced.

I'd soon find out. It was dysfunctional in every possible way. I'm going to talk you through every part of my experience there because I don't want you to miss out on how utterly broken and bizarre every facet of the politics of Stoke-on-Trent was. Everything that could go wrong went wrong – it was beyond anything I'd ever experienced in politics before. Even keen followers of politics and local government are amazed when I tell them about this. So, get yourself comfortable and make sure you've got a bottle of wine close to hand because I'm about to tell you an incredible tale that ends with the unprecedented situation of the post of elected mayor being abolished and me having to attend Belgravia police station, with fellow comedian Jon Richardson, to answer questions about all this. I told you it was going to get mad.

The first thing to understand is that the system was deeply faulty. I don't mean that in a Marxist way, I mean it purely pragmatically. At the time, Stoke was one of only eleven places outside London to move to a system with an elected mayor. Traditionally, local government mirrors the Westminster model. The leader of the council is the leader of whichever group of councillors could command a majority in the chamber. They then choose a cabinet from that chamber to form the executive. So far, so thoroughly normal. The first problem with the elected mayoral model is that there isn't just one. Different areas can choose different executive models. Stoke chose the wrong one. They doomed it from day one. The model they went for was so bad it shouldn't even have been an option.

The most obvious and most democratic model is 'mayor and cabinet'. The public directly elect the mayor, making them more accountable to the public. The mayor then picks a cabinet from the councillors available. So, although the mayor isn't a councillor and is elected in a different way, they still form an executive from the council chamber. Stoke did not do this. Stoke chose a 'mayor and council manager' model. This is where the executive, the people with all the power in the city, consisted of just two people: the elected mayor and the unelected chief executive.

Think of the immediate problems that causes. Firstly, you've just cut the councillors out of the executive completely. No matter what they do, they cannot ascend. They're all stuck down there. You've created a chamber stuffed with enemies who can vote down any of your proposals. Secondly, why create an executive of just two people, one of whom is completely unelected, and therefore unaccountable to the public? If you think the system sounds mad, brace yourself for the politics.

Labour were in a coalition with the Liberal Democrats. It happens. What doesn't often happen is that Labour weren't just in a coalition with the Liberal Democrats, they were also in a coalition with the Conservatives. Yup, all three parties in a triple coalition. It was highly unusual, but you realise how much you have in common with your historic enemies when the BNP start winning seats – the Tory Party suddenly looks hugely progressive compared to them.

This grand coalition of Britain's three biggest political parties was enough to muster a majority of just one seat. One! If just one councillor rebelled or didn't turn up, it was defeat. That would be hard enough if it was only one party running things, but this was an arrangement between Britain's three most famous political enemies. Every day the whole project dangled over the precipice of collapse. The stakes couldn't have been higher. Defeat risked emboldening literal fascists. The BNP had nine seats and the rest of the chamber was a mixture of so-called 'independents' who were hard-left ex-Labour politicians plus some councillors who'd never been in any political party. It was like a bad dream. I used to pray for nightmares when I went to bed just for some light relief.

Stoke is a strange place. Firstly, it's not laid out like other cities, with a centre in the middle and towns and villages around it in a blob. Rather, Stoke is a collection of six towns, all in a row. One of the towns is called Stoke but it's not the centre of Stoke. Hanley is the centre of Stoke. Good luck driving there if you didn't know that. The six towns are locked in an eternal rivalry with each other, usually about who's perceived to be getting more investment than the others. They're not massively keen on their neighbours either, resenting their larger siblings Manchester and Birmingham, usually for a perceived bias in their favour.

While this was true of a large part of the political class, it wasn't true of everyone in Stoke, most of whom are wonderful people. Stoke has a special history of combining industry and design. Stokies have a charming habit of checking any cups and saucers you use in meetings to make sure it says 'Made in Stoke' on the bottom. I only worked there a short while, but I still find myself doing it all these years later. I'd never seen that before and wondered if people in Taiwan did the same with children's toys.

Stoke seemed to exist in a vacuum. The obsession with the six towns being so different did my head in and left me with a life-long allergy to parochialism. It also provided an emotional base for the BNP to build on because that kind of divisive attitude is the first step on the way to nativism. I'd hear this phrase a lot from some councillors and members of the public: 'You wouldn't understand, you're not from round here.' They weren't even saying it to me, they'd say it to each other. I was commuting from Nottingham every day, a whole fifty miles away. If they thought people from the next town were different, I might as well have been from the moon.

Instead of challenging this, weak Labour politicians would agree with it. They were feeding a political culture based on small-mindedness where everything was about where you were from, rather than about how we could work together to solve problems regardless of where we were from. Not only does that argument shut help out, it's ultimately an insult to your own intelligence, because when it is reflected back, you're saying you literally cannot understand anywhere else beyond the place you live. Where does it end? If you're not from Britain, you don't understand? If you're not from England, you don't understand?

If you're not from Stoke-on-Trent? If you're not from Hanley? From Regent Road? Number 5? If you're not from the kitchen? If you're not living in the bin?

Stoke Labour Party was more dysfunctional and antagonistic than a family Christmas with Liam and Noel Gallagher. The factions that Mark Meredith faced could be broken down into three broad groups that overlap in a Venn diagram.

The first group was the resentful hard left. They hated anything Mark wanted to do because he was moderate, young and impressive. They couldn't bear the idea that he might generate some success for the city and were entrenched in a position of permanent opposition to anything he did. They could not be reasoned with, and existed to complain and cause trouble.

The second circle consisted of the jealous. Some of them held or had held prominent positions and felt that they should have been running the city, and they were resentful of the power Mark had. One man in particular was seething that he wasn't leader of the city, so much so that he ran a permanent campaign of sabotage. He was hostile in meetings, constantly leaked things to the media and was endlessly scheming to undermine Mark. Mark is gay, and this man would be openly homophobic, saying behind his back things like, 'I hope he gets AIDS. I wouldn't piss down his throat if his heart was on fire.' It's one of the most shocking and disgusting things I've ever heard.

In the third circle were the weak. Those who could have used their power and position to support someone trying to make a positive change for the city, but chose to keep quiet in case the mob turned on them. In many ways that was the group who infuriated me the most. They would privately agree with you, but then stand by and watch, often because they had worked out that it was advantageous to them not to get involved. Collectively, it was a form of sabotage. It was like being a boxer and having your cornerman tie your gloves together before bellowing instructions to your opponent on where to punch you.

It wasn't just some of the Labour councillors we had problems with. The three local MPs, all of them Labour, were useless in their own special ways. Mark Fisher was the MP for Stoke Central. He was an old Etonian whose dad had been the Tory MP for Surbiton, while his stepmum had been an Ulster Unionist MP and his grandmother was a countess. Which, of course, made him a raving lefty, presumably a form of rebellion he never grew out of. At least it prepared me for the Corbyn years. Mark was permanently pompous and had a knack for finding the point of disagreement in any discussion, like a detectorist on a beach, scanning for coins that would make his wand bleep.

Joan Walley was the MP for Stoke North, also on the left of the party and one of those people who is always in a bad mood. I never met her in a relaxed state; she was always stressed or annoyed about something. It was like she'd stepped on a piece of Lego every morning of her life. I could never understand politicians who couldn't relax in normal company, and I shuddered every time I thought of how she'd talk to the public.

Then there was the MP for Stoke South, Rob Flello. He'd only come in at the 2005 election and along with Mark was meant to be part of a modernising project to improve the local party. He'd only been an MP for two years, but I felt he had already gone native. I didn't get the impression he had the appetite to really take on the hard left or to back Mark up against some of the nastier elements of the party.

The relationship with those three frustrated me more than anything because they were MPs and could have – and should have – used their position of influence for good. A row over reorganising the failing schools in the city was to highlight how badly they let the city down by prioritising their own popularity.

Bad politicians create bad outcomes. Stoke's education system was a disgrace and was totally failing the children of the city. It was in the bottom ten of local education authorities in England and was so bad the government had brought in Serco, a private provider of public services, to run the entire Children and Young People's Services department. There could be no debate about it – the current system was indefensible and needed radical change. Except, incredibly, there *was* some debate about it. The government – a Labour government – was embarking on an ambitious programme called Building Schools for the Future. Under 'BSF', Stoke was set to receive £250 million to build new schools. The government was rightly ambitious and wanted Stoke to submit plans to revitalise education in the city, which included a number of new academies. Even the most average of politicians would have been excited by this. But remember, this was in Stoke-on-Trent.

What should have been a great, unifying project to transform the future of the city instead became a depressing war of attrition. There were some exceptions but on the whole the Labour group didn't like the idea of academies at all. It was like explaining electricity to primitive man. They saw academies as the devil's work. 'I don't want McDonald's educating our kids!' said one. Ronald McDonald would probably have done a better job than most of the schools in Stoke, but I didn't bother to say it. Depending on your view, academies were either a pioneering way to transform failing state schools, setting them free of failing LEAs like the one in Stoke, or a capitalist abomination dreamed up by multinationals to indoctrinate innocent minds. The fire and brimstone predictions about McDonald's and other corporations rolling into Stoke were obviously ridiculous. The truth was far more inspirational: among those interested in getting involved were local automotive companies, building societies and universities. Big local employers wanted to help train pupils so that they could get high-skilled jobs without having to leave the city. This was the sort of world I wanted to live in. Instead of viewing all private enterprise with suspicion, the public and private sector could work together to improve the life chances of pupils. Tragically, it was not a majority view.

Stoke is one of those places where things never go as planned. Instead of having the discussion we were meant to be having – the system is failing and here's a ton of money and reform to build some wonderful new schools, so how are we going to put them to best use? – we ended up being branded as wicked school-haters who wanted to close vital community assets. Of course, some of the schools had to close – they were appalling. But politicians couldn't say that. I remember being at one meeting with a load of parents who didn't want a new school. The current school was failing but they liked it the way it was. No matter how calmly or sensibly the case was put to them, it was no use, they liked the school. Daft arguments began to become the norm. A few parents objected to one of the new schools on the grounds that it was dangerous because there weren't any railings by the road. Even when they received the obvious answer – that railings would be erected as soon as the school was built – they weren't satisfied.

One particular meeting held in a school hall one evening attracted hundreds of parents. The Director of Children's Services was a lovely man called Ged Rowney. He had a softly spoken North East accent and was eternally reasonable. However, some of the politicians and parents became fixated on him. It was vitriolic and irrational. At one point in this huge meeting, one member of the audience said to Ged, 'Point to where the new school will be. Go on, point to where it will be.' He didn't mean on a map. He meant literally, stand in this hall and point in the direction of where the school would be. We were in a school hall, it was dark outside, and I for one had no idea which way was north. This was berserk. We were meant to be improving their children's education, not playing pin the tail on the donkey.

The MPs were no help at all. Despite this being a Labour government working with a Labour mayor to finally give the children of Stoke a decent education, their parochial instincts trumped everything else. Mark Fisher and Joan Walley were against academies ideologically, despite the system they ideologically preferred being a complete failure. Rob Flello was incapable of being supportive. Politicians like that think they're being clever by protecting themselves, but they only defer their own pain. Besides, the city's children had been failed by such dim instincts already, and it was time for those in public office to make the case. To be proper politicians and actually get something done.

The sad truth is that, political differences aside, they just weren't very good. They were below average, so they were always going to make below average decisions. One meeting was particularly painful. We got them round a table in the council with Mark, Ged and a couple of others. The aim was to reach some sort of agreement, however vague, that we could use to show unity and help move things forward. They thought they ran the place, but they had no constitutional power there at all. Mark was being decent in involving them but ultimately the decision was the government's and the council's to make.

That minor irritation aside, that meeting was like the Mad Hatter's tea party, the conversation was so absurd and meaningless. I tried to master a straight, polite expression at all times, regardless of what was being said. I'm afraid I completely failed at one point. We'd managed to agree on a pretty loose form of words that everyone was happy with, which was a rare positive. At this point Rob Flello piped up and suggested that they did an accompanying publicity shot with the press release where the three MPs were dressed as the Three Wise Men. Yeah, fine . . . no, hang on, what? One minute we're in a delicate political situation having to humour some frankly unreasonable individuals and now one of them is suggesting they all dress up as the biblical Magi. Apart from it being a terrible idea, it was also way too flattering. Thanks to those MPs and the others, Stoke never did get the money. The schools were never built. Michael Gove scrapped BSF after 2010 and the £250 million never came. Three Wise Men . . . Those MPs were more like Boggis, Bunce and Bean.

As I said, I would always try and stay calm and civil. I felt it would be easier to build bridges if I was open and approachable. But sometimes I found my patience was really put to the test, especially when Mark was abused for his homosexuality. There was one evening when I secretly hoped he was going to knock someone out.

We were at an event and a man had been stood at the bar all night trying to intimidate Mark by staring at him. It was pathetic, he was behaving like he was in a local pub. At the end of the night we were heading towards the exit and past this tough guy. Mark asked him if he wanted to say anything to him, but he completely bottled it. We walked past him and into the lift. However, just as the doors began to close, the thug shouted, 'Poof!'

That was a mistake. As well as being young and photogenic, Mark also used to be a boxer. He has that calmness boxers have which is far more unnerving than anyone running their mouth off. So quick as a flash, Mark sticks his foot into the lift door to stop it closing. Oh no. He slowly walks up to this chap and squares up to him, even though the guy is a good foot taller than him. Calmly, Mark tells him that if he really does think he's hard, he'll wait for him in the car park. I remember that moment so vividly because that homophobic bully visibly shrank until, the way I remember it, Mark was towering over him. Don't worry, the fight never happened. Mark wouldn't have done it and I'd have intervened to stop it. Well, after Mark had got a jab and a hook in.

I know I'm bombarding you with various strains of bleakness here, but it's all to give you a full appreciation of how deeply broken things were. It's important not to leave anything out, because it explains how the far right was able to gain more power. Let's go back to the three-party coalition we were in. To address the democratic deficit that the mayoral model created, Mark created an advisory board, a cabinet in all but name. It was formed of Labour, Conservative and Liberal Democrat politicians. The benefit of getting talent from different parties meant you had the best the city had. Everyone was making a political sacrifice to be part of it to stop the fascists getting anywhere near running the city. The fear that the BNP would soon control the council chamber was real.

On the one hand, that fear bred a reassuring pragmatism. On the other, the tensions involved in having three parties in a cabinet that wasn't really a cabinet were palpable. The hard left hated the coalition and would frequently accuse Mark and others of 'selling out', even though it had been formed to stop the BNP getting near power.

The BNP had got quite savvy in their campaigning. Many of their leaflets didn't mention race or immigration at all. Some of their leaflets didn't even mention the BNP. They'd pretend to be from 'Abbey Green Residents' Association' and would show local BNP activists dressed smartly raising local concerns about bin collections, dog dirt and speed humps. They were trying to demystify the BNP and pretend that they were lovely chaps really. I am still shocked at how easily they were able to build this reputation for being helpful, concerned citizens, and how gullible some locals were. It was a bit like the Kray brothers helping little old ladies cross the road. This really annoyed me. One elderly man told me, 'They're very nice, one of them even mowed my lawn.' Is that all it takes to enable the far right? He might as well have said, 'I know they're neo-Nazis, but they always say good morning.' What an awful trade-off. I've never thought of the far right as friendly types. They freak me out. Besides, see it for what it is: they're not genuinely concerned, this was part of a simple strategy to ingratiate themselves to enough local people who would then give them a pedestal to spread their message of hate. Honestly, the power of mowing lawns. I suppose they were used to shaving their heads regularly, so it was probably the only transferable skill they had.

As well as the naive, it won't surprise you that the BNP also appealed to the openly racist. Hardly a revelation, but it was a new experience for me. Even in my short time in politics, by the time I was twenty-five I'd been a Labour activist for ten years. I'd campaigned all over the country and, in my experience, it was very rare to encounter someone prepared to either be racist or admit to being racist on the doorstep. Of course, some folk would raise immigration in ways that made you wonder if they were racist, but they realised it made them sound bad so they tried to make it sound respectable.

In Stoke, this was different. For the first time, people would look me in the eye and say they were voting BNP because they hated people from other countries or with different skin colour. This was unlike anything I'd ever known in politics. It scared me. The relative success of the BNP was emboldening racists across the city. If they were comfortable telling canvassers that they were racist, what were they saying in the supermarket or down the pub? What were they doing when they encountered someone who wasn't white? We'd walk down some streets and see window after window proudly displaying BNP posters. I felt like something big was happening and I worried about how we could ever come back from it. It was like I'd woken up inside a Shane Meadows film, but without the jokes.

There was one more type of voter the BNP appealed to. They were what I'd call 'fuck you' voters. They were fed up, wanted to send a strong message and they saw that electing the BNP caused a fuss that voting for the Tories didn't. They wanted to shock the system.

The only thing that got Labour out on the doorstep in some parts of town was the fear of the BNP winning any more seats.

Labour was taking these places for granted. Not so much in terms of policy, but in terms of communication. The party wasn't listening to or talking to them. Labour wasn't visible. This is why campaigning really matters. You have to be talking to voters all year round. Be seen on the doorstep, be face to face with people. The job of a politician isn't just to pop up every four or five years, receive votes and then scuttle back to the chamber until the next election. The job of a politician is to be in continual dialogue with the public, as well as fulfilling your duties in the houses you're elected to. Labour politicians across the UK had only been doing half the job. Of course, there were global economic forces that had transformed Stoke's economy. There was rising concern about immigration and I knew from my experience that most Labour people were squeamish about discussing it, but the biggest killer of Labour in its heartlands was complacency.

What really disturbed me was how comfortable some of the council staff were with those BNP politicians. I'd see staff having friendly small talk with them. While the BNP had done so well, they were entitled to administrative support so some staff didn't have a choice but to deal with them; it was the tone of it that made me uncomfortable. It felt too cosy. Mind you, some of the other people I saw them socialising with were even more surprising.

The canteen at Stoke was a very specific type of bleak. The food was excellent, but the dining area was a dated, high-ceilinged reception room which always felt dark and gloomy. I don't know who was in charge of the music, but I think they were going through a divorce. 'Bad Day' by Daniel Powter was a regular, as was 'Wherever I Lay My Hat' by Paul Young. Both utterly miserable songs. Why would you play that at midday? It created a heavy, melancholic atmosphere. I used to shake it off afterwards by walking round a graveyard to cheer myself up.

During lunch, I preferred to sit in a far corner of the room, eating my dinner and switching off for half an hour, not talking to anyone and just observing my peers. I couldn't be bothered getting lobbied while I was eating. I hated that in office jobs. Just as you are tucking into a baguette you've carefully selected, someone wanders over and goes, 'Matt, have you got five minutes to chat about the report?' Not now, mate, I've got half of Warburton's bakery in my face.

I much preferred looking at the different groups and noticing their interactions. Most people were really friendly towards each other. But one afternoon I had a scan around the dining hall and could not believe what I was seeing.

Sat there in full view of council officers and visitors was one of Labour's most left-wing councillors at the same table as the BNP, eating and guffawing with them. This was a man who used every Labour meeting to lambast the party for being too right-wing. The vitriol he used to spit about Mark selling out to the Tories and Tony Blair being a Tory in disguise was relentless. Yet here he was, having a good old laugh with full-on hard-right extremists. In that moment he exposed what he really was: he wasn't a left-wing man of principle, he was a hypocrite. He was a demagogue and his anger was just make-believe.

When I told other Labour people what I'd seen, most were horrified, but a few tried to make excuses for him. This is how far from acceptable the behaviour of politics in Stoke had drifted. The BNP gave me the creeps; I didn't understand why anyone would want to hang around with them or be seen hanging around with them. But putting emotions aside, I couldn't comprehend how, if your whole identity was being more left-wing than everyone else, you could be joking and laughing with a bunch of fascists over a bacon butty. Oh well, another lesson to prepare me for Labour politics after 2015.

There is a happy ending to this part of the tale. The BNP were eventually defeated in Stoke-on-Trent. To be fair to Rob Flello, he and his office were serious about defeating them and dedicated a lot of time and effort to it. The secret to destroying them was to treat them as any other opponent: expose how lazy they were on the council, tell people how few meetings they'd been to, hold them to account for what dreadful politicians they'd been since getting elected. And doing all of this face to face with locals.

It took proper groundwork, out every weekend, knocking on doors, leafletting estates and taking the message out there day after day. It worked. A few years later there were no BNP councillors in Stoke. The truth about the BNP was that as well as being diabolical extremists, every single one of them was lazy. They weren't real politicians. They were chancers who'd figured out how to manipulate a section of the population for a few years. They had no intention of taking their place on committees seriously or actually changing anything and they were too dim to figure out how things really worked. It was a bit like *The War of the Worlds*. It wasn't firing bullets and heavy artillery at the aliens; it was bacteria that defeated them. Similarly, calling the BNP racists and fascists sadly wasn't enough to stop people voting for them. Highlighting their ineptitude was what did it for them. What a lesson. People in Stoke may tolerate fascism, but they won't tolerate laziness.

The BNP weren't the only ones on their way out. Stoke became the first city to adopt the elected mayoral model and then hold another referendum to abolish it. The inadequate councillors who ran a sustained campaign against the role because they were threatened by it eventually got their wish. The model Stoke originally chose was awful, but it would have been better to move to an elected mayor and cabinet model than back to the leader and cabinet, returning power to the hands of dusty relics, some of whom had only been elected with a few hundred votes. That was always the strongest argument in favour of elected mayors. A mandate. The whole city gets to choose the individual, so it improves accountability. The old way means that councillors can get elected on low turnouts, do a deal with enough backbenchers and become leader of a city with a huge budget when barely 15 per cent of voters in one ward even turned out at all.

And so Mark's position was abolished, and with it, mine. After a few years of intense and extreme experience in politics, I was ready for something else anyway. I'd been talking to friends of mine who were still working for Labour in places like Parliament or head office. They were dealing with different problems – those of a government slowly collapsing. Even though I knew that was deeply stressful too, I'd felt like I was in the middle of nowhere in Stoke, in a world where normal politics didn't exist. That's because I was.

My mate Will Sherlock suggested working in public affairs, where I'd be working around politics, but not in the trenches anymore. I was worried that I'd miss the intensity, but I needed a bit of time away from the front line. I got a job in London working for Consumer Focus, a quango that lobbied government and industry on behalf of low-income consumers, rail passengers and people who used postal services. I moved from Nottingham to London and Stoke was already a distant memory. That was until, during the first week of my new job in the capital, I got a phone call from the police.

The office was just off Victoria Street, close to Parliament, Labour HQ, Tory HQ and various government departments. I loved it. I'd walk down to Westminster Abbey on my lunch break. What a great part of town. Everyone was friendly, I didn't have to worry about internecine warfare and there was a Greggs around the corner. What more does a young man in London want? Well, not to be answering police questions for a start.

I'd barely started in my new job when a colleague told me to check the news because the elected mayor of Stoke had been arrested. I thought he was mistaken but I turned on Sky News and sure enough, it was true. Mark had been arrested on suspicion of corruption in office. I was totally shocked and absolutely convinced that he was innocent. Not just because I'd seen no corruption at all while working for him, but because I knew him and knew it wouldn't be true. I felt for him; what an awful way for his time in office to end. Especially as he was innocent.

A few days later my phone rang. It was the police. They were polite and clear that I wasn't under any suspicion at all, they just wanted to ask me a few questions as a witness. They asked if they could come to the office to speak to me. Politely as I could, I pointed out that I'd just started a new job and it wouldn't look great if during my first week the police were coming in to have a word. We agreed I'd meet them at Belgravia police station. An old pal of mine who still worked for Labour suggested taking along a friend who wasn't anything to do with politics but who was smart and sensible. One man immediately came to mind.

The comedian Jon Richardson and I had been friends for years after meeting at a gig in Nottingham where – and he won't mind me saying this as I told this story at his wedding – he died on his arse. Despite that, it was obvious that he was brilliant and that the audience were wrong. We got on immediately as we had plenty in common – same age, from a similar background, we both loved football and politics, and shared the same sense of humour – and enough that made us different: I'm an optimist who loves life and he's Jon Richardson.

Very kindly, he agreed to come with me. If the coppers recognised him, they didn't let on. He'd started to do a bit of telly but wasn't as well known as he is now. We sat in a police interview room for hours while I answered questions. The issue was about a decision on whether to close a splash pool at a council-run leisure centre to make budget savings. In the end I don't think the splash pool was ever closed. There was a suggestion that Mark had colluded with a local businessman who ran his own leisure centre. I'd seen no evidence of it, and I didn't believe it. I sat in that interview room for hours, with the future *8 Out of 10 Cats* team captain there for moral support. This was around the same time as the 'Cash for Honours' investigation. I got the sense that parts of the police felt that they had to be seen to be taking these things seriously. Which is fair enough, but it all felt a bit dramatic. Just like Cash for Honours, all charges were dropped. Trying to explain politics to the police wasn't exactly easy. They seemed surprised that politicians in the same party wouldn't get on. I had to give them a quick briefing on Labour factionalism and reassure them that loathing people on your own side wasn't just widespread in politics, it was encouraged.

Standing on that balcony at the Royal Festival Hall in 2016, I reflected on my time in Stoke. I'd witnessed parts of the population prepared to send a shockwave years earlier. Once you'd seen people vote for the BNP, voting for Brexit was timid in comparison. To be clear, I'm not saying that voting for Brexit is fascist or extreme. I disagree with it and I think it's against our national self-interest. I think the campaign pandered to our worst instincts around immigration and broke the law. But it's not the same as voting for the BNP. Which I know isn't much of a bar. What I am saying is that I'd seen an appetite for severe rebellion in Stoke and I shouldn't have presumed it would stay there or dissipate forever. The only thing I had an appetite for now, as I stared at the sky in disbelief, was as much whisky as I could find.

Chapter 8

UKIP FM

So many of our current woes can be traced back to the global financial crash in 2008 and the decisions of the Conservative-led government that followed it. A stagnant decade of poor economic growth and in-work poverty created not just long-term economic and social problems, but the perfect incubator for populism. As I'd seen in Stoke and as we know from historic experience with Oswald Mosley, the National Front and the EDL, there has always been low-level tolerance of populism and extremism that suddenly explodes when people don't feel good about their lives.

In the wake of the crash, UKIP started to gain ground, finishing second in the 2009 European Parliament elections. Economic upheaval is the flower bed that allows populism to bloom. Parties like UKIP are the rain that nourishes the seed, even if they think that the rain is God's revenge for gay marriage. I was in a unique place to witness this blossoming.

Before Twitter and internet trolls, there was late-night radio, a lawless platform for loudmouths, weirdos, eccentrics and conspiracy theorists. And that's just the presenters. If you've never listened to a late-night phone-in, then give it a go tonight – it's still a thing for people who haven't discovered social media. If you can stomach the first few minutes, it starts to become addictive. You cannot believe how outrageous and offensive some of your fellow citizens are. The things people are prepared to say on live radio are astonishing; it really gives a unique insight into the darkest thoughts of the British public.

I'd never really engaged with it, but I was familiar with it because my mate Phippsy (real name Edd Phipps, that's how most male nicknames work) was obsessed with Jezza's *Late & Live*, a nightly phone-in show. Jezza was the slightly more imaginative nickname of Jeremy Kyle. Phippsy tuned in every night to laugh at him shooting people down and calling them idiots. It was a skill that made him a millionaire. Jezza, not Phippsy. I also became familiar with the kind of person who would call such shows late at night, because I spent years at talkSPORT hosting the weekend overnight slot.

I was there at a fascinating time, just as UKIP was starting to take off. It was truly eye-opening. I'd left a job where most of my conversations were with like-minded liberal types as well as ministers and MPs. Now my conversations were with people who thought the government put fluoride in the water to control our minds and that 9/11 was an inside job.

Late-night radio had never been an ambition of mine, but

I'd started popping up on these sorts of shows as a guest. Since moving to London for the Consumer Focus job, I'd been able to concentrate more on my main passion: stand-up comedy. I'd done my first gig at sixteen and then dabbled a bit until I started working for Labour and I had no time for anything outside my job. Now that I wasn't working in politics, I could start gigging more regularly. After an Edinburgh Festival run, I'd ended up pratting about on Russell Howard and Jon Richardson's 6 Music show on Sunday afternoons with daft features like 'Fordy's Rumour Mill', where I'd invent outlandish stories about Z-list celebrities. They included Paul Chuckle's sideline as a card shark and ex-Derby player Marco Gabbiadini's hobby as a pigeon-shooting vigilante. It was high-end stuff.

6 Music helped get my name out there and I started being a regular guest on Richard Bacon's 5 Live show and Ian Collins's late-night talkSPORT show. This was radio of a different nature. It was opinionated, confrontational and edgier than anything I'd ever been involved in. After being a guest on election night 2010, talkSPORT offered me the weekend overnight slot. I jacked in the day job and started a new life outside the office. It was like going from riding a rural afternoon bus service through Somerset to getting a night bus in Nottingham. Things were about to get rough.

The hours were inhuman: 1 a.m. until 6 a.m. on Thursday, Friday and Saturday nights. That's not normal. At first, I could handle it, but I quickly hated the effect it had on my body. I was knackered all week and could never adjust to sleeping during the day. I'd have stuff on during the week too, writing on various shows like *8 out of 10 Cats* and *The Last Leg*, as well as gigging a few nights a week. I was in a permanent, shattered trance. I always felt slightly mad, like I'd escaped from somewhere.

On show days I'd turn up at the studio an hour before I was due on. The place was already dead. The first hour or two would fly by, but as the night wore on it would slow down. It was a slog from 3 a.m. to 4 a.m. and there'd still be two hours left. Nevertheless, I enjoyed it. There was a buzz to it all, especially in the first couple of hours. There's something inherently rebellious about staying up late when most people are tucked up in bed – life feels different at night. I never outgrew the thrill that I was up past my bedtime. Plus, I was in my twenties, I was opinionated and full of energy, and I had a platform with a huge amount of freedom. I could choose which stories to focus on and which guests to invite. Labour had not long lost the 2010 election, so the studio I was in turned into a stage from which I could rail against the Conservative-led government and the new direction the Labour Party was taking. Conventional politics wasn't going to feature that much, though; I was about to go down a rabbit hole of conspiracy theories and paranoia. I would encounter obsessions about two issues in particular: Europe and immigration. It was like being at a UKIP conference. Where everyone was smoking weed.

These shows are confrontational by their nature because you're encouraging people to ring in and disagree. You're reliant on callers so any debate has to be framed in a way that makes people feel compelled to call. You can't just go, 'Who thinks the government are rubbish?' You have to hook people in. Let's say you want to start a discussion about committing troops to war. You might start off asking if it's even the UK's role to get involved anymore. The question might be, 'Shouldn't the UK keep its nose out of other countries' business?' It's quite a punchy way to introduce the topic and it'll cut across left and right. If that didn't get many people calling in, you might go further and ask, 'Would you let your child serve in the army?' to make it more personal. Every conversation would go wildly off track. Even lighter topics, like stuff about favourite school dinners that I'd throw in to brighten the mood, would end up with someone telling you whether they'd rather drown or be electrocuted.

A regular caller called Christine would bring every question back to whether God created the world in seven days. One night we were discussing Wayne Rooney's wages and she managed to link it back to Genesis. The book in the Bible, not the prog-rock band, even though that would have made more sense. I can't remember her point now, maybe it was that on the seventh day God rested by watching *Super Sunday* on Sky Sports. Probably on his tablet.

To help me navigate the debate effectively, I had a touch screen to control which callers came on air. They'd ring up and speak to a producer who'd get their name, where they were calling from and a few words about what point they were going to make. It meant I could see which side each individual was on and could bring in different opinions at different times, like the principal conductor of an orchestra. There in front of me was a screen full of people, summed up in a few words. The one I always remember is: *Claire. Watford. I would let a stranger beat my child.* It raised so many questions. Any stranger? For any reason? Also, 'beat'? Why not 'tell off' or 'reprimand'? These were the only people I was speaking to for three days of the week. I had to remind myself that they weren't representative of the wider population, although subsequent events have made me wonder if that's true.

Every show was a study in the success of tabloid propaganda. Every night I'd have a switchboard stuffed full of people repeating back total nonsense they'd picked up via the *Daily Mail*, the *Sun*, the *Express* and the *Star*. Mixed in with the usual hysteria about bendy bananas, banning prawn cocktail crisps and abolishing mince pies was the repetition of invented tabloid phrases. Listeners would regularly rail against 'eurocrats'. It's not an everyday word most of us would use in conversation. It's a made-up, political attack line and shows how powerful the relentless anti-EU agenda had been.

These people were angry about someone they'd never met, someone they couldn't tell you what they did or where they lived or how old they were or where they worked or whether they were good at their job or not. They were getting angry at imaginary people. I met a bloke recently at a football match who was trying to convince me that a No Deal Brexit was a really good idea. The conversation was completely civil and friendly, but when I told him I thought it would lead to job losses – which it already has – he said, 'You're one of them remoaniac snowflakes, you are.'

It sounded so odd to have a tabloid phrase used as if it were a perfectly normal expression. It would be like meeting a date and going, 'Phwoar! Sexy Sarah sizzles in sleek sweater!' You'd sound completely mad.

These guys just didn't like modern life. They thought things were better in the 1950s, even though so many of them weren't even alive then. I'd point out to them that life for working-class people used to be dreadful back then: they lived in worse conditions on less pay and died younger. That wasn't relevant, apparently. Things were better in the past, people had respect and we all knew where we stood.

Nostalgia had been politicised. We lived in an uncertain, volatile world and that was the fault of things like the EU. It's a remarkable feat of propaganda that the EU's greatest success was stability and yet it was perceived by many of my callers as a disruptive force. Peace in Europe was apparently nothing compared to the tyranny of health and safety legislation.

I understood the anxiety of living in a fast-changing world, especially if you were a bit older and if you didn't feel you'd done well out of it. But there was more to their rhetoric – an unpleasant undercurrent of racism. When they talked about life being better 'back then', they weren't thinking about the family unit or the welfare state, they meant you could say what you liked – you could actually say you were a racist. What a thing to yearn for. 'Things were better when I was a lad. You respected your elders, you could leave your front door unlocked and you could be really racist and not get told off.' It was like missing the plague.

If it wasn't racists, it was conspiracy theorists. I'd come across them before: MPs get some weird mail and you occasionally meet a bloke in a pub who thinks he's been abducted by aliens. During every show I'd get calls and texts from people making ridiculous, outlandish claims about all sorts of things. Regular themes included the aforementioned theory that the government put fluoride in the water to control our minds, paranoia about the Illuminati and the Bilderberg Group, and loads of 9/11 conspiracy theories.

This was all underpinned by a general cynicism about anything or anyone perceived to be powerful. I quickly came to realise that some people cannot accept the world they live in. They have to believe that there's something else going on behind the scenes and they'll just make stuff up to support that view. Conspiracy-inclined listeners would even invent stuff about me. They'd claim I'd been privately educated or that I was a millionaire. It was harmless enough, but it was odd. One guy claimed he'd seen me being rude and abusive to bar staff in a Nottingham pub during the 1991 FA Cup Final. A heck of a feat as I would have been eight years old at the time. Mind you, I am from Nottingham, so maybe it's believable.

In opposing the world in which they were living, they were saying something about themselves: they didn't like modern life. For some people it was London, for others it was immigration, for others it was the decline of the high street or globalisation. And this was reflected in the political landscape. I know this isn't true of everyone who voted to leave, many of whom thought the

EU was undemocratic, but Nigel Farage understood the wider cultural context behind the desire to break away from Europe. It's no coincidence that UKIP politicians regularly spouted all kinds of batshit things about gay marriage causing floods or wanting to ban burkas because they caused vitamin D deficiencies. Well, there were two reasons for this: firstly, UKIP politicians recognised that, like a disruptive pupil, if you cause trouble, you get attention; secondly, some of them were crackers. They also did two things. They talked about immigration a lot and Nigel Farage cultivated a persona completely different to the leading politicians of the time.

Nigel Farage may have realised there was a gap in the market, but the other parties were responsible for creating that gap. I felt Labour were more responsible than anyone else. We'd presided over an increase in immigration but hadn't addressed some people's concerns about that – we hadn't sufficiently communicated the benefits of, say, flexible labour. Maybe I'm being too harsh on my own side, but I felt that Labour members and politicians preferred to avoid such a discussion rather than have one at all. I didn't think there was any contradiction in saying that we were pro-immigration and that it hugely enriches our nation, but also accepting that when some areas change, some local people feel anxious and that we should listen to them and reassure them. We should have facilitated a conversation where people could express themselves, however clumsily, and we could have put the compelling counter-argument.

On top of that, we could be seen to be tackling and rebutting the clearly racist elements of the debate. What's definitely true is that not talking about it was hugely damaging. Gordon Brown's encounter with Gillian Duffy, the sixty-five-year-old woman who heckled him and whom he described as 'bigoted', was hugely significant. It suggested Labour didn't understand its own voters. Not just that, it seemed repelled by them. You need to be communicating all the time. You need to give your supporters the benefit of a good argument so that when they're in the pub or at work they're armed with information about why immigration is good. Labour were so good at this when it came to our other achievements and policies; what a wasted opportunity that we didn't do the same for immigration.

An even deeper problem was a total inability to grasp what the growing language around elites and 'the establishment' meant. From 2010 onwards, Labour thought that 'the establishment' was the same old one they'd been railing against: inherited power and wealth. It wasn't. They were completely ambushed by the logic that by being metropolitan, internationalist and politically correct they were part of a different elite. It was that elite that Farage was whipping up dissent against. Attacking opponents like Boris Johnson and Nigel Farage for being posh was pointless and counterproductive. Firstly, they can no more help their background than any of us can. Secondly, it's a cheap shot and looks envious.

More importantly, it totally misunderstood the argument. Leave aside that Nigel Farage and Boris Johnson have an absolute cheek pretending to be on the side of working people, it wasn't that people didn't think they were posh. They clearly are.

They were pushing back against a different elite and Labour didn't realise it was part of it. Farage was able to exploit a myriad of anxieties about life in the 2000s and convince a section of society that it was the fault of the EU and immigrants. I'd speak to Labour politicians about Farage and they just didn't know how to attack him, as if he had magic powers. In a way they were right, because there's no such thing as real magic (apart from Gazza's goal against Scotland in Euro 96). All magic tricks involve misdirection. That's what Farage had mastered.

Farage's persona was a creation, a cartoon character, and it was a deliberate contrast with the stiff politicians he was attacking. They were boring so he was fun, and he was in a pub having a pint. They were serious so he laughed at everything, so that all the photos of him made him look like he had a great sense of humour, while in a pub having a pint. They were earnest, he was pissing himself, while in a pub having a pint. The lesson of Farage wasn't to out-Farage him and start going to the pub to look normal, it was to find a part of yourself you're comfortable with and project your politics through that.

Gordon Brown was best when he made a virtue of being 'a serious man because there's a lot to be serious about'. It was when he felt he had to behave differently that people reacted badly. Crucially, Farage could play by different rules because he wasn't in charge. He wasn't trying to become prime minister so he could be blunter and less nuanced. He's a right-wing populist, it's what they do. He exposed a critical problem, especially with Labour in the post-crash years. They were speaking a different language. And not the sort he'd get annoyed about if he heard it on the train.

If talkSPORT's late-night listeners were a natural constituency for UKIP, Nigel Farage was an expert at cultivating them. He'd be at the station all the time, always available and always full of beans. Energy was his main asset. He was always up for it. I think the public are drawn to the sorts of politicians who are always brimming, always perky, who look like they're enjoying themselves. Tony Blair always appeared as though he enjoyed the job. Boris Johnson always does. Which proves that it's not always a good thing. But when politicians look like they're burdened by office, as Gordon Brown and Theresa May sometimes did, it makes the public feel awkward for them.

I interviewed Nigel Farage a couple of times in those days on the show and my impression of him was that he was an arch Thatcherite who felt the Tories had drifted too far to the left. I think had he risen through the ranks of the Conservative Party, he'd never have left. You could have a good political chat with him because he'd take a point and he had a candour about his opponents and would be generous in his assessment of them. He was perfect for late-night radio. He was opinionated, could make people laugh and had a great voice. He was good at handling people and had fast wits. This was his natural habitat. It's a shame he didn't pursue radio as a career instead of politics. He'd have still been a fucking nightmare, but he'd have done less damage. For all his many faults, faults that I could never get over, he had talent. What a shame that he used it for ill and helped divide and coarsen our country. In later years, the charm faded away and he was left as an angry, bitter man, going to even more extreme lengths to get attention.

Chapter 9

THE DECLINE OF POLITICAL LANGUAGE

The shortage of talent at leadership level has been reflected in the decline in the quality of political language. Politicians are meant to want the public to understand them, yet so often they speak in a language that the rest of us struggle to decipher. Some politicians use phrases not just that no one would ever say, but that no earthling could ever compute, which makes it counter-productive. Here are some of my favourites. By which I mean, these are some of the phrases I hate the most.

'We stand with . . .'

A classic of the Corbyn years. It usually precedes an earnest sentiment about victims of oppression somewhere. As in, 'We stand with the goat herders of Guatemala.' It's not the sentiment that I mind, but if you're a Guatemalan goat herder and Jeremy Corbyn is now standing with you, what does that mean? Is he going to turn up and physically stand next to you? If so, what help would that be? It's the emptiest slogan, appearing to lend support but offering no practical assistance whatsoever. You stand with me. Great. I'm drowning right now, would you mind doing something a bit more dynamic like throwing me that hoop? No. You're just going to stand there. Super.

'For the birds'

I've only ever heard political people say this, and only in the last few years. I infer from the tone of it that it's a disparaging remark about a suggestion, such as, 'The idea that we stand with Guatemalan goat herders is for the birds.' I presumed it was about birds being up in the clouds and somehow linked to that logic, so I googled it. I was wrong. Apparently, it's an old American military term and the original phrase is 'that shit is for the birds', in reference to birds eating horse manure. Which would be much better. I'd rather see an MP on *Question Time* tell the audience, 'Privatise the NHS? That shit is for the birds.' It would be even better if, to honour its origins, they said it in an American accent.

THE DECLINE OF POLITICAL LANGUAGE

'The squeezed middle'

A doozy from the Ed Miliband era. This was Ed's big hit, the phrase that defined his leadership years. It was his 'Wonderwall'. Just like 'Wonderwall', the words are gibberish. It's a reference to the middle classes who apparently felt their circumstances worsen during the coalition years. It was a phrase doomed to never be understood, because it sounded more like a campaign about toothpaste. Which I'd have been on board with. I hate a squeezed middle on a toothpaste tube and always carefully push up from the bottom to extract the maximum available amount. It could have been an exercise DVD – *Ed Miliband's Squeezed Middle* – where you lose weight by doing a sit-up every time you imagined how much better David Miliband would have been as leader. You'd have a six-pack in a day.

'From Durham to Dundee'

Politicians and their speechwriters are addicted to alliteration. It is now impossible for a politician to list towns and cities without using this device. Ian Lavery did it during the 2020 Labour leadership contest, when he supported Rebecca Long-Bailey: 'Labour needs to be formed by working-class communities from Hackney to Hartlepool, from Durham to Dundee.'

The only possible explanation for this kind of stylistic literary technique is that they think it sounds impressive. I'm not sure who is meant to be impressed by this. 'Ooh, he just said a list of places all starting with the same letter. Do you know what, I think I'm ready to overlook the antisemitism and vote for him.' Whenever a politician lists places in that way, 'from Rugby to Ramsbottom, from Ascot to Aintree', I immediately feel all the energy leave my body. Oh no, we've got a bore on our hands. They are to oration what cross-stitch is to knitting. It requires no skill at all, and no one is ever impressed.

As well as being boring, the device has a flaw. If you're trying to list places that start with the same letter, you're not going to get a wide enough geographic spread. Ian Lavery saying that Labour needs to be formed of communities from Hackney to Hartlepool and Durham to Dundee leaves out most of Scotland, the west of the UK, all of the South West, the south coast and East Anglia. Northern Ireland doesn't get a look in.

Incidentally, the Welsh are the best natural orators in the UK and I've never heard a single Welsh politician use alliteration, although it would be a lot harder for them: 'from Llanfair-yng-Nghornwy to Llanfihangel Tre'r Beirdd. From Llanrhaeadr-ym-Mochnant to Llanfairpwllgwyngyllgogerychwyrndrobwllllantysiliogogogoch'.

'Hold their feet to the fire'

Macho slogans are the worst because, on the whole, politicians are dweebs, so it makes them sound ridiculous. 'Hold their feet to the fire' was a favourite of Nigel Farage and Alex Salmond, which tells you everything. Leaders who resort to tough-guy phrases sound bizarre because it's not professional language and it's not something you can deliver on. If Alex Salmond wasn't going to get what he wanted, was he literally going to pin David Cameron down, wrestle him towards the fireplace, remove his footwear and stuff his feet into an open fire? It's such gruesome, medieval imagery. I'm surprised it didn't escalate with Salmond further promising to 'put matches under Cameron's fingernails and light one every time he lies to me. Failing that I'll attach electrodes to his nuts.' It's a slippery slope and it ends up with a politician threatening a rival by going, 'I've got your kids, Dave. I've got your kids.'

'Hardworking Britain better off'

Labour used this slogan in 2014, and just typing it out made me yawn. It's as empty and as pointless as a slogan could get and demonstrates a complete lack of creative talent. You can hear the discussion that led to its creation:

'We need a phrase that tells everyone they'll be better off with Labour.'

'What about "Everyone Better Off With Labour"?'

'Actually, do we want everyone to be better off? Doesn't that make us sound like we're going to make rich people even richer?'

'Everyone in Britain Better Off With Labour. Apart from the Rich.'

'Sounds a bit class war . . .'

'Poor People Better Off With Labour.'

'Sounds like we're rewarding people on benefits instead of those who work.'

'People Who Work Better Off With Labour.'

'It needs to be more patriotic.'

'People Who Work In Britain Better Off With Labour.'

'Ah, you're so close, keep running with it . . .'

'Hardworking Britain Better Off.'

'Nailed it.'

The implicit suggestion is that anyone in Britain who doesn't work hard will be worse off. Given that most of us don't work hard, it's not surprising we didn't like it. It was a personal attack on our way of life.

'Speaks to . . .'

Wonk gold. As in, 'This policy really speaks to the inequality agenda.' Woah, slow down. A policy has developed the power of speech and is talking to an abstract concept? What dimension are we in? This is one of the worst, because it's needlessly distracting and the impact of what's being said is lost. I think what it means is that the policy in question is relevant to and will help tackle whatever it is you're discussing – in this case inequality. So just say that. Stop trying to sound like you're giving a TED Talk and remember that if you want to convince an audience, they have to know what you're talking about. Instead of improving a speech, this phrase makes it worse. It's one of those pieces of verbal signalling that makes people feel part of a club. Like speaking with an inflection or shopping at a farmer's market. Which really speaks to my issues around judging others.

'Putting the government on notice'

A mildly threatening way of telling the government you're holding them to account. Which you should be doing anyway, so what are you on about? You might as well tell the government you're going to sit opposite them. That's what already happens. It creates the illusion of a process. You've said you're putting the government on notice for, say, delivering better GCSE results. If they don't deliver better GCSE results, what are you going to do about it? Er, nothing. Because you can't, because you're in opposition. So why even 'put them on notice'?

It is utterly meaningless, but people like John McDonnell love it because they think it makes them sound tough. Which raises deeper questions about what they're in politics for. Do they want to actually win and change the world or do they just want fans swooning over them going, 'Ooh John, you're so hard putting governments on notice, I bet you're dead strong.'

'The best of us'

There are few experiences more excruciating than a politician trying to sound like a statesperson when paying tribute to someone or something. Let's say it's the anniversary of the birth of the NHS. I guarantee you that a good few politicians will say, 'NHS staff are the best of us.' This may sound harmless enough, but they'll have said it about education staff on another date and about the police later in the year. By definition, if you're saying that one group is the best of us, then you have a hierarchy in mind about how worthy the rest of us are.

Plus, while I take the point that we should all be grateful for, say, NHS staff, not all of them are the best. One or two will be lazy and a few others will probably be bullies. Which would ruin the phrase even more. 'NHS staff are the best of us. Apart from the lazy ones and the bullies. And the ones who nip out for a crafty fag outside A & E.'

'Break the law, don't break the poor'

A Militant slogan that came back into fashion recently. Its only merit is that it rhymes. Beyond that it's terrible. The flaw at the heart of the phrase is that it's not desirable to do either. I'd rather not break the law or break the poor. How have my choices been narrowed to such an extent that there's a zero-sum dilemma between illegal activity and breaking the poor – whatever that means? Militant couldn't even stick to it and ended up breaking both the law and the poor when they passed an illegal budget and had to sack city council staff.

There's a bizarre cheeriness implied by the rhyme, as if it's from a children's book, but its message is about justifying illegal activity. I guess the lesson they learned is you can do bad things if it's got a ring to it. Why not go further? 'Break my eggs and I'll break your legs.'

'The bankers got bailed out, everyone else got sold out'

Another phrase that suffers from being absolute bullshit, so no wonder Jeremy Corbyn loves it. The idea is that when the last Labour government kept the financial services industry afloat to stop TOTAL ECONOMIC MELTDOWN, what Gordon Brown was actually doing was screwing you over and just giving money to bankers for a laugh. The banks were bailed out so that normal people could still access the money in their accounts.

This was about protecting all of us to make sure our bank accounts didn't literally disappear, leaving us with no money, leading to society collapsing and the UK being reduced to a post-apocalyptic hellscape where cannibal gangs rule while the rest of us search for scraps in bins. It's even more irritating that Labour people say this about their own government. It was a rescue package that didn't just help the UK, it was copied around the world and helped prevent a far bigger disaster. But yes,

Jeremy, paint it on a placard and yell it through a loudhailer if it makes you feel better.

'An NHS with time to care'

Ring a bell? You've definitely seen this one written down somewhere.

It's terrible on many levels. As a promise, it's impossible to measure. Whether you think the NHS has time to care or not is a matter of opinion and the pledge itself contains no words to help you understand. Had it been 'NHS waiting times cut in half', that would have made more sense and been quantifiable. The phrase 'an NHS with time to care' also suggests that the NHS is uncaring and, what's more, it's too busy to deal with your silly little problems.

Have one last look at it before we move on and marvel at how it sailed through multiple drafts, decisions and meetings. They thought it sounded good. Then, not only was it printed everywhere, it was carved in stone. Which was a bad idea anyway, regardless of what was engraved on it. It was the political equivalent of the desperate man getting his girlfriend's name tattooed on him so that she doesn't leave. I can't be completely sure Labour didn't consider going that far in 2015 either. I can imagine Ed Miliband taking off his shirt to reveal a huge back tatt listing Labour's six promises.

'Labservatives'

A Liberal Democrat brainwave from the 2010 election. I loved how awful it was so much I printed it off and had it on my desk at work. Every day I would gaze at it, mesmerised by its crapness. In case you can't figure it out, it was the Lib Dems' ingenious way of suggesting that because Labour and the Conservatives always won the election they were somehow on the same side – i.e. no matter who you vote for, the Labservatives always win.

There's so much wrong with this it's hard to know where to begin. Let's deal with the logic first. Everyone knows that Labour and the Conservatives are mortal enemies, including the public. They have a bigger gap in ideology between them than either of them do with the Lib Dems.

Then there's the fact that the word itself is a mess. Labservative. It's clumsy to say, looks terrible written down and doesn't work as a pun. I suppose it was either that or Conbour. If they did it as Tories, they could have had Laries, which sounds more like a sign of the zodiac, or Torbour, which sounds like strong continental lager.

The irony is that after the 2010 election the Lib Dems went into coalition with the Conservatives and are still dogged by accusations that there's no difference between them and the Tories. Which is unfair. But slightly enjoyable.

'A future fair for all'

I always misheard this as 'a future free-for-all', which made it sound like life under a Labour government would be like one massive school canteen food fight. Sadly, it wasn't to be as exciting as that.

This was the title of Labour's 2010 manifesto and was accompanied on the cover by a cartoon of a sunrise, which made it look like a box of cereal. Fairness was the in word around 2010, but it was eternally problematic because it means completely different things to different people. You might think that community service is a fair punishment for littering, whereas I'd go slightly further and say that a fair punishment would be the death penalty. Campaigning on a word like fairness makes you sound like you're whining to your mum about having to go to bed early. 'Muuuum, it's not faaaaaiiiir!'

'Change that works for you'

The Lib Dems' uninspiring 2010 general election slogan. Change is going to work for me? What, change is going to turn up Monday to Friday and I have to employ it? Hello change, thanks for showing up, would you mind starting by hoovering the flat?

It's meaningless. They'd have been better off not having a slogan. This is the sort of empty phrase that could be used by any organisation in any sector. If anything, it sounds like some sort of spare change charity campaign run by a supermarket: ASDA – making change work for you. No voter has ever said, 'You know what I really want? Change that works for me.' They'd have been better off with 'Lib Dems: We'll Tidy Up All the Dog Shit'. Because that's what voters actually say they want politicians to do.

'Brexit means Brexit'

Simply repeating a word does not define it. If this was an equation, it would be Brexit = Brexit. Which is like saying 5 = 5. Which is pointless. You'd just write 5. It's the same here: Theresa May would have been better off just saying 'Brexit'. It was particularly frustrating as it was the biggest issue facing the country since the end of World War II. An entire nation was on edge wanting to know exactly what leaving the EU was going to mean. Leavers were worried it would be fudged and that it would somehow involve staying. Remainers worried that we'd completely burn our bridges with Europe and isolate ourselves in the world.

Into this heated arena walked a new prime minister tasked with solving this problem and who invented a phrase that barely deserves the title. It's three words and two of them are the same word and that is itself a made-up word. It's a riddle that cannot be solved. Worse still, it reminds me of that awful expression, 'We are where we are.' Yes, I can see where we are, I'm here. Or as they'd say, 'I am where I am.' It's the verbal equivalent of a shrug.

Chapter 10

THE CURSE OF COMPLACENCY

Over the last few years, you'll have found yourself remarking to friends about how mad politics has gone and wondering aloud how we got here. Shortly before bursting into tears and reaching for the revolver.

Political chaos doesn't come out of nowhere, much as it can feel like that. The global financial crash is a big part of it, but we also arrived at this situation because two politicians took big risky decisions that put our stability at risk: Ed Miliband changing the leadership rules of the Labour Party – 'one member, one vote' – in 2014 and David Cameron holding the EU referendum in 2016. In doing so, each in their own way put their party before their country. A critical mistake.

What is remarkable about both these decisions is that the huge risks were blindingly, terrifyingly obvious. The flaws had already been proven. David Cameron came too close to losing the referendum on Scottish independence in 2014 and Ed Miliband led a party that had almost imploded in the 1980s due to hard-left entryism. Yet that did not stop them. Both men were complacent about the magnitude of what they were about to unleash, and their decisions have had a catastrophic effect on the country.

I became increasingly annoyed with politics during the coalition years, mainly because the two major parties weren't doing what they should logically have been doing. Ed Miliband was indulging the Labour left, which is knowingly election-losing behaviour and therefore completely irresponsible. The Conservatives had modernised, but only a little bit. After years of irrelevance they still couldn't bring themselves to do what was required to win. Had David Cameron really modernised his party, instead of giving it a cosmetic rebrand, I'm convinced he'd have won a majority of his own in 2010.

Why, you might ask, did I even care about the Tories? They're not my team; it would be like getting annoyed about Poland's defending at the World Cup. I cared because even if I'm not going to vote for a party, they're still affecting the world I live in. If they behave irresponsibly, we all feel the consequences. Pour yourself a whisky, you're going to need it. More, more . . . just a touch more. Let's go.

Also, and please don't punch me, but I liked David Cameron. After years of the Tories drifting further to the right, it was refreshing to see them choose a socially liberal leader. He came across as moderate; he had talent and he was gracious to his opponents. He'd given Tony Blair a standing ovation after his last PMQs, something not every opposing leader would have done for a rival. When he first became prime minister, I was struck by his praise for the Labour government he'd just removed:

'Before I talk about that new government, let me say something about the one that has just passed. Compared with a decade ago, this country is more open at home and more compassionate abroad and that is something we should all be grateful for and on behalf of the whole country I'd like to pay tribute to the outgoing prime minister for his long record of dedicated public service.'

Maybe I'm just a soppy git, but I feel emotional reading that tribute again.

What concerned me about Cameron and his party was that he hadn't the guts to take on the Eurosceptic right properly. The comparison is always going to be Clause IV (when Tony Blair dropped the commitment to nationalisation from the Labour constitution), but those big symbolic moments tell the public that you really have changed. Cameron hadn't had one such moment. He tried with Europe, but that ended up being a retrograde initiative, by taking the Conservatives out of the European People's Party grouping in the European Parliament. It removed the Tories from the main centre-right group in Europe, which included Angela Merkel and Nicolas Sarkozy. An early and ominous warning sign for what was to come . . .

Generations of Conservatives had slagged off the EU and helped create a solid base of Eurosceptic opinion in the country. Incredibly, some of these Tories were pro-Europeans who did it to curry favour in the party and thought that trashing the EU didn't really come at a wider cost. It's a fact that will never stop blowing my mind, up there with Loch Ness being able to hold the world's population ten times over. Because in politics, every word has an impact somewhere. Contributing to a relentless stream of Eurosceptic propaganda would obviously generate hostility towards the EU. That's what Cameron had done. During the 2005 leadership election he promised to withdraw from the EPP to head off the apparently surging Liam Fox. If I had been Cameron, I'd have given the Tory right something else and pledged to bring back fox hunting. Starting with Liam. The desire to fox hunt is so strong in the party, both Fox and Hunt have stood for the Tory leadership, although tragically never on a joint ticket.

After taking the Tories out of the mainstream centre-right group in Europe to fend off Liam Fox, Cameron then promised an in/out referendum on our membership of the EU to fend off Nigel Farage. The poor thing must have felt like he was in a zombie film, having to distract the undead with buckets of entrails. Although that would have been a massive improvement on what actually happened. At least zombies don't skull a crate of Stella and congregate in Parliament Square while chanting, 'We want our country back!' I'm not pretending that doing the opposite wouldn't have come at a cost for Cameron, but given the choice between having a hard core of rebellious Tory MPs constantly causing trouble and threatening to sabotage their own government on one hand and being the prime minister who took the UK out of the European Union when you wanted to keep the UK in the European Union on the other, I know which one I'd take. It's like being given the choice between suffering a constant headache for the rest of your life and having your head amputated. Yes, the first one will make your life hell and yes, the second course of action will cure the first. But you'll be dead.

The main problem I had with him calling the referendum was that he actually wanted to stay in the EU. The best way to do that was to not have a referendum. If I wanted to have spaghetti Bolognese for dinner, I wouldn't do a Twitter poll where the two options were spaghetti Bolognese and gravel, I'd just have spaghetti Bolognese. What Cameron did was give himself two options: spaghetti Bolognese and Never Eat Spaghetti Bolognese Ever Again. Just don't take the risk! His defence was that he had to call the referendum because he'd promised it to the public and he didn't want to break his promise. Without sounding like the totally cynical git that I definitely am, he should have tried to find a way out. Say the circumstances have changed, say you want to deal with the deficit first, say Dennis Hopper has strapped a bomb to your chest and if you hold a referendum it will explode. Say *anything* to try and get out of it. That course of action would not have been without significant upheaval, so I'm not pretending it would have been easy. But when you're prime minister, you have to put the welfare of the country above everything else, including party and personal issues. That's what the job is all about.

Cameron's Massive Mistake Number 2 was the way the campaign was fought. Vote Leave did absolutely everything in their power to win that referendum, but Stronger In were restricted by Cameron's desire to hold the Conservative Party together. Vote

Leave didn't seem to care whether the Tories survived or not and spent the entire campaign telling lies and indulging in personal attacks. They had all the discipline of a stag do approaching midnight. Imagine if Stronger In had been allowed to fight back and do whatever it took.

I understand the calculation, given that everyone thought Remain were going to win. But never fight a half-arsed campaign. Stronger In weren't fighting with one arm tied behind their back, they were fighting with both arms tied behind their back and their legs strapped together while blindfolded and wearing a ball-gag (which some Tory MPs used to be into). I never understood how they didn't change their mind during the campaign. Once again, I understand the high ideals and the importance for a prime minister to keep their party united, but once Boris Johnson, Michael Gove, Priti Patel and others started trashing their own government, it was naive and complacent not to fully respond. They should have unloaded on Boris Johnson, running powerful attack ads calling him out for being the liar that he is.

David Cameron had an opportunity to build a new coalition of centre ground voters as Jeremy Corbyn was leading Labour. Maybe it's fanciful to think that there's a world in which Cameron goes all out to win the referendum, succeeds and then wins over a load of moderate Labour voters who were disillusioned with Corbyn. But if there's a world where that happens, that means there might be a world in which Nottingham Forest actually gets promoted to the Premier League. I choose to believe.

It's not all David Cameron's fault. Woah now, put the cricket bat down and hear me out. It's *mainly* his fault, but others should also take responsibility for their role in the defeat. Jeremy Corbyn, a lifelong Eurosceptic, was a constant problem. Vote Leave knew they needed to convince Labour voters, hence the use of the NHS as their main campaign message. Labour voters needed to hear from their leader about why they should vote to remain. What they got was a grown man, a would-be prime minister, having a public strop. His resentful tone at the events he bothered to attend, his immature refusal to share a platform with the other parties, his confusing 'remain and reform' message and his ridiculous answer that he was '7, 7 and a half out of 10' for staying in the EU all sent a clear message to Labour voters: it's OK to vote Leave. The leader of the Labour Party didn't even lead Labour's campaign.

It was left to Alan Johnson, who hadn't been on the front bench for six years, to lead Labour's campaign. In an email to supporters in the wake of the defeat, he said of Corbyn's office: *At times it felt as if they were working against the rest of the party and had conflicting objectives.*

That's putting it politely. Can you imagine any other recent Labour leader letting someone else lead the party's campaign in such an important vote? OK, maybe Ed Miliband, but that's not the point.

Ah, Ed Miliband. Ed the Enabler. I know some people get very upset when Ed Miliband is criticised, in the way they do if someone is cruel to a kitten. At least a kitten wouldn't have dog whistled to the hard left* and then changed the rules to allow a party with a history of entryism to be completely taken over by a sect determined to destroy it. Ed did. It was one of the most destabilising decisions taken by a modern British politician, and it triggered a process that led to Labour becoming completely irrelevant and nasty. Ed Miliband isn't just responsible for the election he lost as leader, he's also partly responsible for the two that Jeremy Corbyn lost. He emboldened the hard left when he was leader, handed them the kingdom and set Labour on a course of self-indulgence. He was the gateway drug, the cannabis to Corbyn's crack cocaine. I often wondered if he was smoking it, given some of the decisions he took.

Ed Miliband's crucial flaw is that he thinks the hard left are actually quite good. He likes them and he wishes he'd been more left wing when he was leader, despite a mountain range of electoral evidence to the contrary. A lot of the soft left feel like this: they admire the angry radicals who get up and shout, they envy the energy and passion, they romanticise going on marches, waving placards and banners, and they forgive the authoritarianism, economic illiteracy and bullying. This is because they admire ideological dedication, like churchgoers who wish they had the commitment to become a nun. In their world, knowing every tiny detail about the history of the left is currency.

There's nothing wrong with that if you're running a radical book group. But when you're running the Labour Party, it's a

---

* It's probably impossible for a kitten to dog whistle.

distraction. That's where their mind is, not on how to win elections so that you can improve lives, but how you can convince yourself that being really left-wing will somehow pay off this time. And if it doesn't pay off, who cares? At least you stood up for what you believed in.

This is one of the most indulgent instincts in Labour politics. Losing is a nightmare for the people who really need a Labour government. To see victory as an optional extra is missing the point of why Labour was formed as a political party in the first place. It was formed to get into government, not to be a vessel for political vanity. How ironic that those most obsessed with Labour history are those who ignore its most important lessons.

Lessons like the experience Labour had with Militant, a vicious Trotskyite entryist group which tried to take over the party in the 1970s and 80s. Their aims and values of revolutionary socialism were completely counter to those of the Labour Party, a democratic socialist party. The long battle to remove them, epitomised by Neil Kinnock's rousing speech at the 1985 Labour conference, made Labour look like an ungovernable rabble. Labour would never have won an election again if Militant weren't kicked out. Like their descendants Momentum, they flooded Labour branches and tried to bully existing members out. They intimidated people, weren't afraid to be physically abusive and were effectively a hooligan element.

Ejecting them took years and scarred the Labour Party. It was a deeply distressing episode that influenced the Labour Party rules in the time that I was working there. In the DNA of the party was the fear of it happening again. Strict rules governed the smallest of selection processes, built so that branches and constituencies couldn't be swarmed again. I learned about Militant in retrospect, so it's incredible that a man who'd lived through it at the time would then make it so easy for the hard left to take over the party again. The complacency of it was frightening.

The hard left are like the Terminator. They cannot be reasoned with. And they'll nationalise your clothes, your boots and your motorcycle. They exist to be extreme; they get off on it. They have to be the angriest people in the room. The idea that there's a world in which Militant and New Labour types could ever sign up to the same agenda is ludicrous. Yet it's what Ed Miliband believed. Why a party should try and accommodate a group of people who want to destroy it never made sense to me. You might as well tell airline pilots that they should be more open-minded about terrorists. You can't get along with a group of people whose politics is extreme and whose behaviour is disgraceful. Organisations like Militant and Momentum are aggressors. They exist for conflict. Which makes the admiration of them from elements of the soft left so bewildering.

In fact, it's worse: there are sections of the soft left that are more sympathetic to the Corbyn project than the Blair project, even with all the havoc it visited upon the party and the successive victories it handed to the Tories. They feel more like they're from the same tribe, that they're similar types of people. In a way they are – they're people who will always lead Labour to defeat.

For the five years that he was leader, Ed Miliband didn't just distance himself from the most successful period in Labour history, he made it OK to slag it off. It had taken Labour twenty-three years to win an election again after their last victory in 1974. Labour was losing for eighteen years because they weren't listening to the public. Labour finally won again, three elections, two of which were landslides, because they figured out that to win you have to be in tune with real people, not just the ideologues in your own party. When Labour politicians trash the last Labour government, what they're really saying to the public is, 'We're going to ignore you.' It's therefore no surprise that the public return the favour. After the Tottenham riots in 2011, Ed Miliband was interviewed on Radio 4 and said: 'I deeply regret that inequality wasn't reduced under the last Labour government.'

There are at least two problems with that statement. Firstly, Labour weren't even in power at the time of the riots. Yet here was the then leader linking the outbursts of violence to the last Labour government. Secondly, he blamed the 1997–2010 Labour administration for the riots by claiming that it had not reduced inequality. In other words, it wasn't really a Labour government at all. In moments like those, he was helping contribute to Corbyn's rise. He tickled the tummy of a slumbering beast, something which fairy tales tell us is a very bad idea.

Anyone with even the vaguest memories of the Blair and Brown years will know that his statement was factually incorrect. The minimum wage and tax credits helped reduce economic inequality. Historic investment in the NHS helped reduce waiting times from over thirteen weeks to four weeks, and improvements were made in cancer care and tackling heart disease, which reduced health inequality. The huge leap in educational attainment, which meant that in 2010, 76 per cent of English pupils were achieving five good GCSEs compared to 45 per cent in 1997, helped reduce educational inequality. The removal of the homophobic Section 28 led to a reduction in inequality based on sexuality.

All of this is not just stats and facts; every one of these represents many lives that were improved. People from backgrounds like mine who were given a better chance to make something of themselves. People with cancer who were diagnosed more quickly, which meant they could live longer, healthier and happier lives. Trashing that record does no good to the Labour Party at all and it must strike the public as odd. They were Labour's best years since Clement Attlee. Here's another football analogy: it would be like Manchester United fans constantly attacking the record of Alex Ferguson and thinking David Moyes was a genius.

The danger of not listening to the country is fatal for political projects because they can't succeed without winning elections. Parties that can't handle public opinion have a choice. They can either learn from it and change, reflecting more the needs and mood of a country they seek to govern. Or they can dig in and find reasons why the public is wrong. That path isn't just suicidal, it's toxic. What many supporters of Ed Miliband and Jeremy Corbyn have in common is that they don't really like the UK that much. After the 2015 election you may have seen a Miliband fan on BBC 2's *Daily Politics* struggling to process the defeat. He had a tantrum and complained that, 'This country doesn't deserve a leader who's got so much, like, integrity and principles. I think Ed Miliband's too good for this fucking country.' In that moment he summed up how so many of them felt. They're better than us. They understand things and we don't. They genuinely believe that if only the feckless British masses would stop reading the *Sun* and swilling Carling, Labour would win every time. Their vanity prevents any serious reflection. They can't be wrong, they read the *Guardian*.

All of this was crucial in handing the leadership to the hard left. Just as important was the normalising of poor leadership. Ed Miliband simply was not good enough to be prime minister. Persisting in selling him as a statesman was humiliating for the party and insulting to the country. The public was telling Labour that they wouldn't vote for him and the party ignored them. Labour, apparently the party of meritocracy, was telling the country that substandard leadership was acceptable. People rightly expect their prime ministers to be impressive individuals. Obviously, Boris Johnson challenges this logic, but he was up against Jeremy Corbyn, so the point stands. All the arguments that Corbyn's fans made about his incompetence had been rehearsed under Miliband. The most prevalent is that a total lack of charisma is a positive thing for a leader.

This is berserk. Leaders need to inspire and convince nations in order to win and deliver change. You can't do that without a level of charisma. If you choose someone who isn't charismatic, it's an admission that you've chosen a weak candidate for factional reasons. Most of the time it's a defence of a poor candidate, but if you actually believe stuff like that, you're on your way to becoming a flat earther. You might as well argue that a total lack of arms is a positive thing for a goalkeeper (sorry, I can't help myself).

The cultural shift away from a winning mentality was bad enough, but the decision to change the leadership rules was catastrophic. It was now easier to choose the leader of the Labour Party than it was for you to select a local council candidate. You didn't have to have been a member for six months, you could just rock up, pay three quid and change the course of history. In other words, you didn't need to be emotionally invested in the fate of the party at all.

Having run various selections, I thought it was insane. It went against everything we'd been trained to be vigilant about. The potential for entryism was huge. Labour was actively inviting mischief, but there was one small safety valve in the process. To get onto the shortlist which any old sod could then vote on, candidates had to receive nominations from at least 15 per cent of Labour MPs. In 2015 that meant getting thirty-five MPs to nominate them. Given the complexion of the parliamentary party back then, it should have been enough to prevent any hardliners getting onto the ballot paper.

It wasn't. Because Ed Miliband wasn't the only one who was complacent. A cohort of Labour MPs who should have known better decided to put a Marxist on the ballot paper to 'broaden the debate'. If they wanted as broad a debate as possible, they must have been gutted they couldn't find a fascist.

Politicians who indulge in this behaviour think it makes them look magnanimous. I think it makes them at best daft and at worst reckless. It would be like campaigning to keep your local police station open by signing a petition to close it. It's all to curry favour with the party, to look like a good guy. Labour needed politicians with guts who could tell their own supporters difficult truths, not those who would fail in their basic duty as gatekeepers. The phrase I heard a lot was, 'I'm going to lend my vote to Jeremy', as if it was a book they were going to get back.* You don't lend a vote, in the same way that you don't borrow a sandwich. Many of those MPs were immediately remorseful when he won, but it was too late. They'd been warned and they hadn't taken it seriously. Like Ed Miliband, they thought we were overreacting. They were disastrously complacent. John McTernan, Tony Blair's former political secretary, called them 'morons'. It was a label Margaret Beckett agreed with, which was a bit of a surprise as she was one of them.

---

* Don't go lending this book out to your mates, make sure they buy their own copies. They'll never give it back and I've got bills to pay.

Chapter 11

THE COLLAPSE OF THE CENTRE

Political parties often go mad, but they usually have the decency to take it in turns. The election of Jeremy Corbyn as Labour leader in 2015 followed by the Tory civil war after the 2016 referendum meant that both government and opposition were imploding at the same time. Both major parties had been captured by their populist fringes. This was profoundly destabilising for the country because it meant the mainstream of British public opinion had been deserted by our two major parties. Millions of us felt politically homeless and still do. It ruined my relationship with the Labour Party, and it will take more than a new leader to repair it.

I can only imagine how voters who didn't have the emotional connection to Labour must feel. I think it will take a long time to get them back. While the blame has to lie with the populists and those who enabled them, there are also lessons for those of us who've been on the outside the last few years. What could we have done to stop this madness and what can we do to prevent it in the future? Well, there are a number of options, one of which involves violent retribution. But let's discount that for now.

Discipline is crucial to sustained political success, but finding the right balance is difficult. A total lack of discipline is a nightmare and repellent to the public. It also damages a party long into the future. It was twelve years after Neil Kinnock's heroic 1985 conference speech that Labour won in 1997. Once you lose the public it takes you a long time to get them back. Some dissent has to be allowed, not just because it's part of a healthy democratic debate but because it can help improve policy. It also shows the public that parties can accommodate different ideas. If you go to the other extreme and pretend that you all agree on absolutely everything, you end up like the SNP, where their MPs had to sign a loyalty pledge, which means they can't 'publicly criticise a decision, policy or another member' of the group. Given how some SNP politicians have behaved in recent years, that's turned out to be unreasonably restrictive. Although perhaps it explains why they needed it in the first place.

New Labour were seen as the masters of discipline. A typical caricature of New Labour MPs had them chained to their pagers with fear, such was the ruthless command and control structure enforced by Alastair Campbell. It's not entirely inaccurate, although it will have applied more to ministers than MPs. Given what had come before, Labour had to be disciplined and be seen to be disciplined in order to win.

However, in one crucial area they failed. Left-wing MPs were allowed to vote against the Labour whip in Parliament repeatedly without serious sanction. One of those MPs was Jeremy Corbyn, who voted against his own government 428 times. That is an industrial scale of rebellion. Carlsberg don't make cantankerous backbenchers but if they did, it'd be Jeremy Corbyn. These serial rebellions were when Labour was at its most popular, so he was proving himself out of step not just with his party but also with the country.

I understand why he wasn't chucked out. It looks bad to remove what appears like a harmless lefty, it inflames the local party, other MPs would have been in uproar in solidarity and you'd have created a problem in the constituency where he might have stood as an independent and taken the seat from Labour. However, you would also have sent a message to other dissenters that rebellion on that scale is unreasonable and has to be punished. Crucially, you would have ensured that hardcore socialist elements weren't in a position to take over the party again. The other benefit is that it reminds the public that Labour has changed for the better and that you're more concerned with the country's priorities than those of some crusty Marxists.

The most important lesson I've learned from Labour's decline is that even at the height of success, the argument is never fully won. You only ever win the argument temporarily. Unless you think about it like this you inevitably become complacent. The challenge is to win the argument and then keep winning it again and again over a sustained period of time. This requires constant communication. You have to keep telling the country and the party what you've achieved – both electorally and in policy terms. In every interview, at every event and at every party meeting, everywhere, remind them all what a Labour government is doing about the things they care about. Plaster the facts everywhere – best ever GCSE results, best ever A-level results, devolution, longest period of economic growth, peace in Northern Ireland – over and over again until you get sick of saying it. Of course, as you achieve more, you add the new successes to the list and keep reminding the party and the country that you can only have these things if you keep winning.

This is repetitive, so it can quickly become boring and opponents will take the piss, but don't let that put you off, own it. 'I just want to start by saying something I know you're already sick of hearing, but under this government we've had the longest period of economic growth in our country's history. I also want to tell you that I've loved you from the moment we met. Will you marry me?' OK, maybe don't do it everywhere.

There are two audiences for these messages. The country needs to hear you promote your record because they need to know what you're doing in office. Most people aren't using every public service at the same time, so they might not know about what you're doing for schools, say, or to prevent the rise in crime. The party needs to hear you promote your record because they need to know that only when they remain near the centre ground are these progressive successes achieved. Remind them that when the left were in charge they never won an election and weren't able to do anything. Remind them that every time the left has run the party, the Tories get in and destroy everything that Labour governments have achieved.

Fusing success and values is vital for reminding members what politics is about. The Labour Party was founded to be a party of government, so winning is a Labour value and you can only implement other Labour values when you win. Losing is a betrayal of the founding principles of the party. That's why it's not a think tank or a pressure group. When it becomes a vessel for the intellectual vanity of indulgent men – as we saw with Miliband in the last chapter – they're the ones who should be regarded as sell-outs, not those who do the hard work of winning rare election victories. Of course, some people inside and outside the movement will never be convinced. There's not much you can do about that, but you can't let it stop you. If you don't defend your record, no one else will.

The other challenge is that a new generation of members brings new perspectives. Even at a young age, I'd seen how hard it was for Labour to win and what they'd had to do to get those victories. Tony Blair had been an inspirational figure to me because he was the one who'd finally beaten the Tories. But the generation after mine grew up with Blair as a figure to rebel against, whether for Iraq or tuition fees or whatever other issues a prime minister becomes unpopular for after ten years. This isn't wholly true, of course – there are plenty of young people who do realise Blair's talent and achievements and plenty of older people who don't. But it was a common conversation with young supporters of Jeremy Corbyn who thought Tony Blair was a Margaret Thatcher figure and anything he'd done had to be bad.

I've spoken to various young Corbyn supporters who are convinced that Jeremy was crucial to securing peace in Northern Ireland. I have to gently point out that no, he wasn't, and that it was actually his nemesis Blair who achieved the breakthrough. Jeremy had been nowhere near it, for good reason. He was a backbench MP so had he been in any of the meetings, he'd have had to scale the perimeter fence, dodge security and clamber in through a window. Secondly, he wouldn't have been an honest broker as his loyalties were on one particular side, the side which just happened to have links to the IRA.

The point is, never underestimate a new generation's ability to learn a different lesson from your experience. That was the direct price paid for Labour politicians deserting their own record. When successive Labour leaders and politicians have attacked the party's time in office, why would anyone who wasn't around at the time think any different? Well, they could look it up for themselves, but at least make it easier for them.

The Tories faced a similar but different problem. They started to erode in office, and it was only Labour having bigger problems that kept them in. It's what won them the 2017 and 2019 elections. Never mind 'Get Brexit Done', their slogan should have been 'We're Shit and Mad, But We're Not As Shit and Mad As Them'. In just over a year the Conservatives went from winning an outright majority with David Cameron in May 2015 to total civil war in the referendum of June 2016. The behaviour of the pro-Brexit wing was disgraceful. They didn't care about the party at all. What they really cared about, what they'd joined the Tory party to achieve, was getting the UK out of the EU at any and all costs. They used David Cameron as a human punchbag and called their own government liars. They were prepared to burn the house down.

The implications of the lies told in that campaign will have profound effects in the future. Whether it was about our financial contribution to the EU or the economic impact of leaving, when the reality turns out to be different, the sense of betrayal will rise. That's something for the Brexiteers to own in the future, but in the years that followed the immediate result, they began to change the Conservative Party into something different. Something worse. Yes, I know this now sounds like a trailer for a horror film. In a way it is.

You can say many things about the Conservative Party, and I have. All the stereotypes about them being selfish bastards and only being on the side of the rich have some truth in them, but there's also another side. There's always been a strong emphasis on public service and most Conservatives care about society and helping those at the bottom more than you might think. I don't think they're dedicated enough, but I know plenty of Tories who have just as much of a social conscience as some Labour people. They're less antisemitic too. Moderate Tories have a very strong sense of duty and are aware of the importance of parliamentary democracy. They were genuinely concerned about Labour's problems under Corbyn because they understood the importance of a strong opposition and they worried about what their own side would do when faced with such an appalling opponent. They were right to worry. There's no way Boris Johnson would have become prime minister were it not for Jeremy Corbyn. That doesn't absolve the Tories for choosing him, but it's the context in which the decision took place. When Johnson became prime minister, I remembered a New York taxi driver I spoke to before Trump's election. He was supporting Trump and when I asked why, he replied, 'Because crazy times need a crazy guy.'

I disagreed. Surely crazy times need a sensible guy to stop the crazy times. And sensible times need a sensible guy to stop them going crazy. In fact, there's never a good time to put a crazy guy in charge (and anyway, we've had plenty of guys in charge, let's have more women – Labour have still never elected one to lead them). Trump and Johnson are very different characters, but they're expressions of the same problem: both the Republicans and the Conservatives have been bewitched by a seam of libertarianism that thrives on a culture war. Their instinct is to divide rather than unite. The UK is leaving the European Union at a time when Putin is hacking elections across the world and China is becoming more powerful. This could not have happened at a worse time. A country of our size should be grouping together with other similar-sized democracies to resist those dictatorships.

Instead, we're going to isolate ourselves. Boris Johnson chose which side to campaign for in that referendum based on his own selfish desires. He didn't care about the geopolitical impact of us leaving the EU, or the jobs that will be lost, the homes repossessed or the risk of breaking the peace in Europe, he just wanted to become prime minister. His little plan worked, so whoopee for him.

He's not good enough to be our prime minister. He's not on top of the detail because he's not bothered about it. The rest of his government follows suit. He has a history of saying awful things about single mums, black people, Muslims, gay people and various other groups. The things he's said are completely reckless and show him as a man willing to make cheap attacks on people who can't defend themselves. He's a glorified school bully, picking on those he thinks won't hit back to make himself feel better.

I accept that he makes the Tory Party feel good about itself and that on occasion he can make the rest of us laugh. But it's not a comedian we need, it's a proper leader. The fleeting moment that Johnson makes people feel good is nothing more than a sugar rush. It doesn't last and a few moments later you crash and feel worse than you did before. Plus, it doesn't contain any nutrition and puts further strain on your arteries and heart.

Some days I can't believe he's the prime minister. It's like I've forgotten. I'll turn on the news and he'll be giving a statement and I'll think, *Fucking hell, he's actually in charge*. Then I'll stare out of the window all day, mind totally blank. He's a lazy blagger who thinks he can just breeze his way through life. Sadly, he's been proven right. Although if he'd have grown up on the same street as me, I don't think he'd have got very far. He'd have ended up as a pub bullshitter, running his mouth off and having kids all over town. Ah . . .

If we want to stop people like Boris Johnson and Jeremy Corbyn taking over our parties again, we have to learn from them. Sadly, the clear and obvious fact they're both totally incapable hasn't been enough to stop party members choosing them. This means that as well as appealing to people's heads, we must also appeal to people's hearts. It turns out it's not enough to let facts speak for themselves, you have to emotionally move people. I always feel conflicted by this. I'm a bit of a soppy sod so I don't mind a bit of heart, but I wish that it wasn't necessary. Politics would be a lot easier if party members were more rational. In different ways, Boris Johnson and Jeremy Corbyn were able to do this for their own audiences. Johnson dazzled the Tories with entertainment, Corbyn stirred Labour by invoking past struggles. Labour loves nothing more than getting emotional about struggles, even ones they know little about.

Brexit is the ultimate example. There were many flaws with the Remain campaign, mainly that supporters were hindered by Cameron's desire not to retaliate, but where was the emotional case to Remain? I don't think it would have been wise to make the emotional case for the EU and get all soggy-eyed over how wonderful Brussels is. Brussels are? No, that's the food. Is. There should have been more emotional advertising about how patriotically British it was to stay in the EU. 'Land of Hope and Glory', Stuart Pearce and Winston Churchill in a Hurricane plane drinking pints of Bombardier as they fly over locals playing cricket on a village green before swooping across the Channel to stick it to Hitler. I'm just spitballing here. OK, never let me near a major campaign. But you get the point. Stronger In was very effective at highlighting the genuine economic risk of leaving the EU, but it didn't stir the soul. There was little or no appeal to the heart.

Vote Leave ran a highly emotional campaign. In fact, it went beyond emotional, it was inflammatory. They stirred up irrational fears about Turkey joining the EU (still hasn't happened) and 76 million Turkish nationals being able to move here. Apparently, Michael Gove now regrets this. Tom Baldwin asked him if he wished he hadn't pandered to 'low sentiments' over Turkey and Gove replied:

> I know what you mean, yes. If it had been left entirely to me, the Leave campaign would have a slightly different feel. I would have to go back and look at everything I said and think whether that was the right response at the right time. There is a sense at the back of my mind that we didn't get everything absolutely right. It's a difficult one.

Now that he's all grown up, Michael can see the error of his youth. After all, he was only forty-eight back then, a spring chicken, he couldn't have known any different. Let's learn the right lessons from his experience. Appealing to people's heart as well as their head is good. Making up lies about foreigners is bad. It's very bad.

Anna Soubry, the former Conservative MP who left to join the Independent Group (who then changed their name to Change

UK and then changed their name to the Independent Group for Change) told me a brilliant story about how she dealt with concerns about immigration from local residents. Pay attention, as this is a masterclass in using facts to make the emotional case for something. When constituents would say they were worried about 'all these illegal immigrants', she'd get out her pad and pen and ask the person which illegal immigrants they meant because if they were illegal, they needed reporting. She'd theatrically spin around as if hordes of illegal immigrants were going to amass behind her. The person complaining didn't mean illegal immigrants, of course; this was Anna's way of getting them to be more honest about what they really meant. Sure enough, inevitably, they'd admit it wasn't illegals they were annoyed with, it was just that they didn't like Polish people.

This is when the masterstroke was deployed. Anna would ask them if they knew the local cemetery. Often they knew it very well because they'd have a loved one buried there. 'The reason that cemetery has so many Polish graves in it is because Polish people who lived round here fought side by side with us to defeat Hitler.' Wallop.

Chapter 12

THE RISE OF POLITICAL BULLYING

I got bullied a bit at school. It happens to quite a few kids, so I don't want to make a big deal out of it, but it left me with a lifelong loathing of bullies. The feeling of being singled out, of being scared to fight back, of being powerless is totally crushing. Internet trolling is online bullying. Watching people revel in the denigration of other human beings reminds me of the sensation I had when I was surrounded and knew I was about to get a kicking. I could feel my pulse pounding in my ears. I was desperate for someone to walk past, see what was happening and intervene. On social media the pile-ons are visible, but too few of us rush to the defence of someone, particularly if we disagree with their views.

Bullying has been normalised within our political culture. We've accepted nastiness as part of our political discourse, and we shouldn't. We excuse as passion an aggressive outburst against an opponent we don't like, and we turn a blind eye. Some of us would be horrified to think we're bullies, but we might even dip our toe in a bit and say something nasty about a politician just to get some sweet retweets and likes. Ooh, that felt good, I had a pop at Chris Grayling and got three more followers, I should do it more often.

We don't just want to best our opponents in a debate or exchange, we want to hound them, humiliate them and destroy them. Politics doesn't exist on an island – well, it does in Britain – but it's a symptom of a wider societal problem about harassment, particularly online. We've begun to reward political bullying and it's ruining people's lives. I say we – I mean you. I don't get involved in that sort of thing because I'm better than you, you Tory bastard.

Insults and protests have always been a part of politics. 'Tory scum' isn't a new phrase and even the word 'Tory' itself is an old Gaelic insult for 'robber' or 'outlaw'. Which makes them sound way cooler than they are. Perhaps they were the opposite of Robin Hood, robbing from the poor to give to the rich. Anyway, this is quite enough Tory bashing and I'm undermining my own point.

It has gone further than that with mainstream parties, particularly Labour, the Conservatives and the Scottish National Party, failing to control their own supporters. The first event of this new era was the Scottish independence referendum of 2014. So much of what happened during that campaign was new in UK politics, particularly the proliferation of online campaigning, the use of social media, the rise of new media and allegations of Russian interference. While friends of mine who support independence understandably found it inspiring and invigorating, my friends on the other side of the divide had a different experience. Which is a heck of an understatement. I might as well have said that Jesus had a different experience to the onlookers at the crucifixion. Which is a bit of an exaggeration, because in the independence referendum no one got crucified. Well, not literally.

I should disclose at the start of this that I'm not a supporter of Scottish independence. I have many good friends who are, including some in the SNP. I totally understand the emotional pull of it, especially when I'm in Scotland. It's an amazing place with wonderful people, including my girlfriend, so I'd better watch my mouth. It's one of the most beautiful countries on earth with stunning natural scenery, crisp, clean air and tap water that's actually drinkable. There's whisky everywhere, the pubs stay open really late and haggis is one of the best foods ever invented. Did I mention that the people are amazing?

But loving Scotland and agreeing with independence are two different things, whatever the hardcore nationalists would have you believe. The emotional argument in favour of it is the most compelling – that Scotland is a great country capable of running its own affairs. I'm not unsympathetic to the argument; it's just that, like Brexit, I think the price to be paid for it is too high. Economically, it's worse than Brexit. In 2018–19, Scotland received £2,000 more per head in spending than the rest of the UK. In the last financial year, the Scottish government raised £63 billion in taxes, but spending for and in Scotland was £75.3 billion, a £12.3 billion deficit. That year, the Scottish government's deficit stood at 7 per cent of GDP compared to the UK government's deficit of 1.1 per cent of GDP.

Leaving that relationship would clearly create an economic upheaval for Scotland. What's patriotic about putting your own people out of work, having them sell their homes and close their businesses, and the effect that would have on their life chances? I suppose I could ask the Brexiteers, but economics isn't exactly their forte.

This isn't a competition. There are years when Scotland has been a net contributor to the UK and that may well be the case again in the future. Even though the economic impact of the coronavirus may make those differences in deficits seem almost irrelevant, the point is that for the years when any nation in the UK has a less strong year than their other partners in the Union, we have each other's backs. Through the pooling and sharing of resources, we all have a buffer to insulate us against our lower-performing years. This isn't about saying one country gets a better or worse deal, as that will ebb and flow in different ways over the years. It's that, by partnering with your closest allies, you have a stronger economy and society.

Independence campaigners said they'd keep the pound in 2014, now they want an independent Scotland to have its own currency. This requires building up huge reserves of currency first, which means spending less of what you bring in on your citizens. So, a newly independent Scotland would have to face a huge shortfall in spending and be putting billions aside to prepare for a new currency. On top of that, borrowing will be more expensive for an independent Scotland than it is for the UK, backed by the Bank of England. In short, an independent Scotland would start life with a programme of austerity that would make George Osborne look like some king who'd gone mad and showered his subjects with gold. That may sound daft, but it's more realistic than the SNP's predictions about how much oil money there'd be to pay for a new independent country.

Facts about economics appeal to the head but as we know from Brexit, you've got to appeal to the heart too. The arguments in favour of independence are fundamentally emotional. Brexit is a growing problem for voters in Scotland. They voted to remain in the EU and yet they're going to have to leave because of the way voters across the UK, including majorities in England and Wales, voted. It would annoy me too.

It's not just the democratic problem it poses, it also appears to say something about the values of our countries. In short, it suggests that Scotland is more open, tolerant and internationalist and that England is closed, intolerant and nationalist. Leave aside the irony of a nationalist party offended by nationalism, this is about the people rather than the politicians. Plenty of 'No' voters feel like the UK they signed up to isn't the one they've now got. They worry about England; they think we let them down. At times I'm minded to agree. I don't like the Brexit result any more than they do, and we've all had to reassess the country that we're living in as a result.

But the UK and England didn't suddenly change on 23 June 2016. Like every country, we have our problems and that referendum helped expose them. There's lots about this country I don't admire, but let's not pretend that England is some uniquely awful place, defined only by its xenophobes. And anyway, not every Brexit voter is some statue-defending lobster. England is a diverse, complicated, wonderful and infuriating place to live. We are people. Beautiful, varied, contradictory, irritating people. I'd put myself more in the irritating camp than the beautiful camp, by the way. But then, you already know that, you saw me on the front cover.

The people of England and Scotland are so much more than the results of elections and referendums, where we're forced to make imperfect choices between substandard options. They shouldn't be hung over our heads as proof that we're selfish English Tory bastards or mad raving Scottish nationalists. The idea that the two countries are completely different with irreconcilable differences is ludicrous. We're as similar as any two countries could possibly be. We don't just share an island, we share language, culture, currency, families and friends. We laugh at the same things, we go to the same festivals, we all like a drink. I find it emotionally distressing when we're pitted against each other or when I hear people, apparently sensible, thoughtful people, talk about England like we're the source of all the world's problems. Often these people will be English themselves, but that's for another book.

The conundrum I've not had a decent answer to is this: if leaving unions is such a bad idea, why repeat the mistake? The best answer I ever get is that 'the two unions are different'. They're right, but not in the way they think they are. Scotland trades four times as much with the rest of the UK than it does with the whole of the EU. Anyway, I don't want this to become a manifesto. These debates are often emotional and don't always benefit from facts or reason, so I've tried to quickly set out some of the main issues I have with independence so that when we get into the problems I had with the campaign, you know where I'm coming from. I'm not a Little Englander and I'm not someone who thinks England is better than Scotland because I don't believe that to be true. I am someone, though, who, like I said before, has a Scottish girlfriend who's going to pay particular attention to this chapter so has to be very careful about how he approaches this subject. In short, I don't want to get my nuts cut off. Wish me luck!

The 2014 independence referendum was a firework display of emotion, propaganda and social media storms. It was the first democratic exercise in the UK that really felt like it was being fought online. So many of the themes and language in our politics, including those that ran through the Brexit campaign and the rise of Corbyn, started in that referendum.

The first, and most obvious, is the use of the phrase 'Project Fear'. Apparently, it was an ironic phrase used internally by Better Together that leaked out. Alex Salmond pounced on it. It was used by the nationalists as a way to dismiss mainly economic concerns about voting for independence. Standard Life say they'll leave? Project Fear. BP and Shell say your oil reserves will run out faster than the SNP are telling you? Project Fear. Scotch whisky producers are worried about a future currency and its effect on their industry? Project Fear. Instead of addressing legitimate concerns, that attack line denigrates the people who are worried. It says that they're scaremongering, they're talking the country down. They're not patriotic. It may sound familiar. Two years later Vote Leave would weaponise the same phrases and sentiment. If you were worried about your job, you were talking Britain down. The problem for those who've used the phrase in the past is that on Brexit, the concerns are turning out to be Project Fact.

Vote Leave learned a lot from the Yes campaign. As well as using their phrases, they also saw how effectively the SNP had put the NHS at the heart of the referendum. I'm sure you don't need me to tell you this, but the NHS in Scotland is fully devolved. It is run completely by Scotland and rightly so. But in the 2014 referendum, the Yes campaign realised they needed Labour voters in order to win. What do Labour voters care about most? The NHS. So, despite the obvious flaw in the logic, they told the people of Scotland that the NHS was on the line. The Scottish government claimed that 'wholesale privatisation' of the NHS in England threatened the Scottish NHS. It's incredible that a referendum about wanting autonomy should concoct a row about areas where autonomy already existed. You're reading this in at least the year 2020 so you know what happens but, brace yourself . . . the NHS in England has not been privatised 'wholesale'. Who knew? (We all did.) Two years later we went through another referendum where lies about NHS funding were used to get Labour voters to vote to leave a union. They borrowed so many of their ideas from the SNP I'm surprised the big red bus wasn't tartan.

The BBC is a relentless problem for politicians because it's impartial and the best news outlet in the world. It employs some top-class journalists who rigorously hold politicians to account. As a result, politicians of all parties attack it. The BBC is not perfect and sometimes it gets things wrong because it's run by human beings. Politicians, who, it is important to remember, are also human beings, should be allowed to complain and to receive an apology if they've been misrepresented. There is a line, though. If you wage all-out war on the BBC, you are attacking our only impartial news organisation. If you trash them because you don't like the questions they're asking you, you do lasting damage to their ability to report the truth. Whenever a political movement goes to war with the BBC, ask yourself why – it's usually because it cannot stand having the truth told about it.

Sure enough, in 2014 the SNP's approach to the BBC was thrust into the spotlight. The BBC's Nick Robinson had asked everyone's favourite embodiment of decency, Alex Salmond, two questions. He answered one and not the other. When Nick Robinson pointed this out, he was accused of heckling Salmond and was then promptly booed by an auditorium of the first minister's fans. That looks bad enough, but the following day 4,000 independence supporters marched on the BBC's Glasgow HQ demanding that Nick Robinson be fired. It was shocking. The intimidation of journalists, especially in this way, should have no place in a democracy. And where was the outrage in the nationalist community? Which leading voices appealed for calm and distanced themselves from this sort of mob intimidation? Salmond himself called the protest 'civic and joyous'. Oh yeah, it was a right laugh for the BBC staff inside, I bet it was like a carnival for them.

Nick Robinson wasn't the only victim of the most horrendous bullying during that campaign. Jim Murphy, one of the leaders of the 'Better Together' campaign, had to suspend campaigning after being attacked by increasingly hostile yobs. As well as sabotaging his events by screaming over him, they pelted him with eggs in Kirkcaldy. In a sign of things to come in left-wing discourse in the UK, one Yes supporter held up a placard which read *Jim Murphy – War Criminal and Supporter of Apartheid*. For the record, Jim Murphy is neither a war criminal nor a supporter of apartheid, but you probably already knew that. I wonder how the Yes campaign would have responded if this was happening to Nicola Sturgeon.

Friends of mine had horrific experiences. I know at least two people who were spat at in the street, one of whom was called a 'traitor cunt' in front of his children by the bloke wearing an SNP badge who'd spat at him. Clearly elements of the nationalist community felt they could do what they liked and get away with it. Years of hate were unleashed during that campaign, often by apparently progressive people. It wasn't just 'Project Fear' that lived on after 2014. A lot of the behaviour we saw in that referendum inspired bullies that followed. Labour supporters of the Union were branded 'Red Tories', a term of abuse that supporters of Jeremy Corbyn gleefully used against anyone in the party to the right of Corbyn. Which back then was quite a few people. Even the Yes campaign's response to the harassment of Jim Murphy was that it condemned 'all forms' of abuse. A gloriously Corbynesque answer. They might as well have blamed it on Tony Blair for a full house.

The most pernicious aspect of nationalist bullying is the suggestion that any Scot supporting the Union isn't actually Scottish. It's built on a desire to rob their opponents of their identity. I cannot imagine how emotionally exhausting it must be to have to put up with this sort of undermining behaviour. Revelling in Labour's collapse in Scotland at the 2015 election, Alex Salmond said that Scottish Labour 'wasn't Scottish and wasn't Labour'. Apart from being intellectual crap, this was a political heavyweight gaslighting a section of the Scottish population. Some people in politics don't just want to defeat their opponents, they want to demoralise and humiliate them. The basis of this and the 'Red Tory' abuse is the suggestion that agreeing with the Tories on the Union is incompatible with being a progressive.

What does it say for the SNP's assessment of the Scottish people? Do they think Scotland is so unreasonable and unsophisticated that it can't understand why politicians from different parties would sometimes agree on something? Of course SNP politicians will work with Tory politicians on particular issues, so it's deeply disingenuous to use occasions where people do agree with Tories as proof that they're wrong. Besides, thinking that calling someone a Tory wins an argument is something you should grow out of by the time you're sixteen, not fail to realise by the time you're first minister.

The 2014 referendum was a turning point for our political culture. Mainstream politicians had allowed their most aggressive supporters to do what they liked. Things have got worse since, which is why some leading voices in the nationalist community have started to call out the abuse. I should make it clear, I'm not talking about the majority of supporters of independence. I know lots of people who still support Scotland's independence and they're amongst the most wonderful and decent people I know. It's a hard core of activists I'm talking about, which sadly is still a lot of people.

The people inside the movement who dare to challenge them deserve our support. Angus Robertson, who was so masterful as the SNP's Westminster leader he was effectively the leader of the opposition, has started telling the movement hard truths about its behaviour. It's a hugely welcome move. I've had tons of abuse on Twitter from Scottish nationalists (and Corbynistas and Brexiteers). It's always disappointing when they go unchallenged by their own side. It's also important to remember that I have brilliant exchanges and friendships with independence supporters online (and Corbynistas and Brexiteers), so it's not all bad. The abuse, though, is counterproductive, which is a good reason for movements to get their own supporters in line.

In a BBC Scotland documentary about the referendum, Stewart Kirkpatrick, who ran the Yes campaign's digital output, admitted that the behaviour of some supporters had been detrimental to the cause. He said, 'The cybernat thing definitely hurt us. Unequivocally. People being abusive online did not help the Yes campaign.' Sadly, we still have a way to go. During the coronavirus pandemic, the SNP's leader in Westminster, Ian Blackford, retweeted a mocked-up road sign at the English–Scottish border that said *We're shut. Fuck off.* He commented above it: *Perhaps not the language I would use but for some folk perhaps it needs to be blunt before they get it!* It's not so much a dog whistle as a wail to the wolfpack. A few weeks later a group of extremists were removed from Glasgow Central station for abusing passengers alighting trains from England. They carried a huge banner that read *England. Get out of Scotland.* Nicola Sturgeon regularly warns politicians from other parties to watch their tone lest their words inspire undesirable behaviour. While she's not responsible for the behaviour of a band of pillocks, she should ask herself whose side they're on and why. It's not the evil Tories.

Successive movements have copied the 2014 blueprint: unleash hell online, say whatever it takes to win, trash the BBC and humiliate the enemy. Nuance, reason and decency are out. In 2015, when Jeremy Corbyn became Labour leader, this went to the next level. The behaviour of some of his supporters was so severe he was forced to ditch his 'Kinder, Gentler Politics' slogan because it had become a punchline. Corbyn's supporters denounced anyone in the party who didn't like him as a 'Red Tory' or 'Blairite scum'. The tone of the Labour Party descended the moment Corbyn became leader. Notable Corbyn supporters openly bullied people online. If you dared disagree with the project, you could expect to be insulted as a 'melt', 'slug' or 'nonce'. Apart from being terrible and counterproductive behaviour, this wasn't the great rebellion they thought it was. Mainly because calling someone a melt stopped around the year 2004. They might as well have accused their opponents of being fans of The Rasmus – they're not words that mean anything anymore. It was a clique of nerds acting out their fantasies. They were pretending to be tough, like those schoolboys who pretend they've had sex with a really beautiful girl from the year above but, er, she doesn't go to this school anymore and, er, her dad will beat up anyone who talks about it.

Anyone who wondered if Corbyn would deliver a kinder and gentler politics quickly got their answer when he hired Andrew Fisher as a senior adviser. Fisher had campaigned for the hard-left party Class War at the 2015 election. As their name suggests, they're an immature and thuggish outfit who vandalised Liz Kendall's office when she lost to Corbyn in the leadership election. Fisher was on video saying of former Labour minister James Purnell: 'I had the most excruciating half hour of my life where I was sat in a room with James Purnell. I still have nightmares – very violent, bloody nightmares about it, fantasies possibly . . . It took every sinew of my self-discipline not to thump him.'

This normalising of violent language was typical on the hard left and immediately contradicted Corbyn's claims of being a man of peace. If he really cared about creating a more pleasant politics, he would not have hired someone like Fisher in a senior position. Campaigning for other parties is against Labour rules so Fisher was suspended when a tweet surfaced telling voters in Croydon South to vote for Class War at the general election. Fisher's suspension was magically lifted so he was allowed to be hired. Compare that with the way Alastair Campbell was expelled from the party for admitting after an election that he'd voted Lib Dem and the whole hypocrisy of Corbyn's leadership is exposed. Like the tyrants the hard left lionise, it's one rule for them and one rule for everybody else. It was to become the defining theme of the Corbyn project. Well, that and total ineptitude.

The petty nastiness, online bullying and hypocrisy were bad enough but something far worse accompanied Jeremy Corbyn's leadership – antisemitism. When I worked for Labour, I'd occasionally hear members say things at meetings and events that were prejudiced. I heard misogyny, homophobia and racism. Not a lot, but I'd overhear the occasional comment from a member in informal settings. It would always shock me that Labour members could hold such views. One thing I never encountered was any antisemitism or conspiracies about Israel. Maybe I didn't work for the party long enough. Maybe there were comments and I didn't pick up on them, but in the years since I've racked my brain trying to recall even the slightest signal. I honestly can't remember any. Like many people, the first time I really became aware of the severity of it on the left was under Corbyn's leadership. Which makes sense, because none of the other Labour leaders in my lifetime had been knocking about with Hamas and Hezbollah. The two tend to go together. Whatever I think of Ed Miliband, I'd never suspect him of being pals with the IRA.

A sympathetic analysis would be that Labour had 300,000 new members join in quite a short space of time and that some of them were a bit wacky. Even if there's an element of truth in that, why were so many wacky people keen to join Labour under Corbyn? It was simple – he'd been aligning himself with extremists and saying appalling things for years. As the country slowly started to educate itself about Corbyn's history, it was appalled at what it found. In 2012 an artist called Kalen Ockerman created a piece of antisemitic street art in east London that featured Jewish men with big noses playing Monopoly on the back of the world's poor. It also included other conspiracy tropes – masonic symbols and reference to a 'new world order'. The moment you see it you recognise the propaganda. It's shocking. After locals complained about it being racist, it was going to be painted over. Ockerman complained about his art having to be removed on Facebook. Jeremy Corbyn replied: 'Why? You are in good company. Rockerfeller destroyed Diego Viera's mural because it includes a picture of Lenin [sic].'

Good company. Wow. I think I'd have gone with 'Bloody hell, it looks racist to me', but hey, that's Corbyn for you. In 2018, the then Labour MP for Liverpool Wavertree, Luciana Berger, asked why Corbyn had responded in such a way. Corbyn said: 'I sincerely regret that I did not look more closely at the image I was commenting on, the contents of which are deeply disturbing and antisemitic.'

To be fair to him, we've all commented on some racist street art we didn't look at properly while being a Labour MP and then made up a bullshit excuse about it when we became leader of the opposition. There but for the grace of God.

The use of the word Zionist has become a dog whistle for those who want to say things about Jews but don't want to appear racist. But don't take my word for it, Jeremy Corbyn accepts this and said himself: 'I am now more careful with how I might use the term "Zionist" because a once self-identifying political term has been increasingly hijacked by antisemites as code for Jews.'

So why did the leader of the Labour Party admit he had to be more careful in the language he used? In a 2013 speech he'd berated some 'Zionists' he'd encountered at a previous event and then added: 'Having lived in this country for a very long time, probably all their lives, they don't understand English irony either.'

This from a man whose supporters claimed was the least racist man to ever live, and yet he was saying deeply offensive things about people from a different ethnic group. Imagine if he'd said that about black people. It would be seen for what it is. Imagine if he'd rung up LBC and said that about Indian people. Well, he'd be given his own show, but that's not the point.

There are so many examples of things Corbyn has said and done that are deeply offensive. He sponsored a parliamentary motion to rename Holocaust Memorial Day as Genocide Memorial Day,* a motion that was tabled on . . . Holocaust Memorial Day. He's thoughtful like that. Or the time the Labour Party wanted to adopt the International Holocaust Remembrance Alliance's definition of antisemitism in full. Corbyn wanted to amend it to include an extra passage containing the phrase: 'Nor should it be regarded as antisemitic to describe Israel, its policies or the circumstances around its foundation as racist.'

Corbyn was voted down and those diabolical words were not included. It's incredible that during a debate about antisemitic abuse, Corbyn was lobbying to be able to say that Israel's very existence was racist. This wasn't the Labour Party that I'd worked for, this was a party becoming a vessel for cranks and conspiracy theorists, not to mention anti-Jewish racists. I cannot imagine the emotional pain that Labour's behaviour has caused the Jewish community these last few years. Watching from the sidelines, it's been horrific to see good people treated with such disdain. It's been emotionally distressing witnessing people who needed support from their party having to get support from the police instead.

---

* https://edm.parliament.uk/early-day-motion/42381. It's still there in all its glory on the parliamentary website.

The worst abuse was reserved for Jewish women. Luciana Berger, Ruth Smeeth, Margaret Hodge and Louise Ellman were all Jewish Labour MPs targeted by Corbyn's trolls. I know Luciana and Ruth. They are both brilliant, talented and decent people. I cannot believe how strong they were in enduring the endless stream of violent abuse they received. In normal times they'd have been prominent members of Labour's shadow cabinet looking forward to a future in government. They are both immeasurably more talented and gifted than Corbyn. Instead of being given the platforms that their talents deserved, they became targets. Watching them get bullied was sickening; the lack of humanity they were shown by Labour was a disgrace. A party that trumpets its principles of solidarity, not to mention anti-racism, left innocent women to the mercy of a racist mob.

Both of them needed police protection because the abuse they faced was so appalling. Luciana even needed it at the Labour conference. Her local party, overrun with Corbyn supporters, tried to deselect her when she was at her most vulnerable. Ruth received over 25,000 pieces of racist abuse in a single weekend and needed police protection. Saint Jeremy, the man who loved to quote Desmond Tutu – 'If you're neutral in situations of injustice, you have chosen the side of the oppressor' – didn't speak to Luciana or Ruth during their ordeals. Not once. The leader of the Labour Party deserted Jewish women when they needed his help and protection. What a lovely bloke.

The scale of the problem, and the extent of Corbyn's denial of it, were exposed in a powerful *Panorama* documentary. Members of Labour staff, some of whom had joined the party because they were inspired by Corbyn, revealed the truth about the culture he'd presided over and the torrent of anti-Jewish racism being spouted by his supporters. Supporters who were not being punished by the party. The whistle-blowers were clearly emotional; it had taken a lot of courage for them to speak out. The most powerful testimony was from Sam Matthews, Labour's former head of disputes, who said he'd become so frustrated he'd actively considered suicide.

So, did this make Corbyn and his cronies stop and think about what they'd done? Is the Dalai Lama a Catholic? Labour's response was horrific. The official line under Corbyn was that the allegations came from 'disaffected former officials' opposed to Mr Corbyn's leadership who had 'personal and political axes to grind'. Labour's manifesto was committed to ending the use of non-disclosure agreements so surely it would be hypocritical and unethical to use them on their own staff? Corbyn's lot didn't think so and got Carter Ruck – one of the most powerful legal firms in the world – to enforce them by sending threatening letters to Labour Party staff. Labour, the party of the workers. As long as the workers keep their mouths shut about what the bosses get up to.

I know one of the whistle-blowers. Mike Creighton was one of Labour's most respected members of staff when I worked for the party and was known as an all-round political brain. He's always open and approachable and wears his wisdom lightly. He's sharp, funny and gentle. I couldn't believe it when I sat down to watch *Panorama* and saw him on it. He ended up being director of the disputes team while Corbyn was leader and he recalled a story about Seumas Milne asking his advice on what to do about antisemitism. Mike told him that they should deal with the top-level cases swiftly and robustly and that Corbyn should make 'a significant speech on the issue of the Middle East and simply say that Israel had a right to exist'. Milne's response was to laugh in his face. It hurt me knowing that a decent, talented member of staff who'd given his life to the party and was giving excellent advice was being humiliated in this way by someone above him who didn't have a clue about how to run a political party. That's bad enough but the implication of the laughter is that Israel having a right to exist is somehow funny. I wouldn't open with it.

The documentary also exposed what people like the historian Dave Rich had been telling the public about Corbyn for years. The company he kept was often extreme. According to *Panorama*, Sheikh Raed Salah claimed that the Jews were behind 9/11 and called them 'germs of all time'. He's a hate preacher and no sensible person would want to be seen anywhere near him. Jeremy Corbyn did, so the point remains intact. Corbyn is on video in 2012 telling Sheikh Salah that he is invited to the Houses of Parliament: 'You will be assured of a very warm welcome. I look forward to giving you tea on the terrace because you deserve it.'

Tea! This isn't a hard-nosed 'we have to talk to people we disagree with in order to achieve peace' stance, this is two friends having a natter over a cuppa. You know how it is: how's the wife? How was the holiday? The Jews were behind 9/11. No doubt Corbyn got his favourite biscuits in, too. Unless they're seen as decadent capitalist filth these days, I can't keep up. I'm not sure extremists are the biscuit type, but then I didn't expect them to drink tea either. Professor Alan Johnson, author of the report 'Institutionally Antisemitic: Contemporary Left Antisemitism and the Crisis in the British Labour Party', says that whenever Corbyn had things Salah had said relayed to him, his justification for seeing him was that 'he didn't say anything like that to me'. This is the ultimate wilful ignorance. I'm not buried under Fred West's patio, but I know he did it.

Labour's problem with antisemitism was so deep, it was investigated by the Equalities and Human Rights Commission. The Commission has only investigated one other party in its entire history and that was the British National Party. You'd think that would have been enough to prompt some introspection. When you're in the same category as the BNP, you might reassess your behaviour. It's like someone saying, 'You know who you remind me of? Hitler.' You'd start to wonder if perhaps your behaviour had become a little extreme. Maybe you'd go for a pint with a mate and ask them to give it to you straight. Not Jeremy Corbyn. Instead of looking inward, his response was to attack the EHRC. In the 2019 general election, Corbyn pledged to make the EHRC 'truly independent', an open threat to the commission that if Labour won, it would transform it. It was a bold strategy to respond to claims of bullying by bullying the people investigating the bullying.

I know this chapter has been a bit heavy. It could have been a lot heavier, but I didn't want to completely depress you. While I always try and be fair in my assessment of people and parties, that doesn't mean turning a blind eye to appalling abuse. All parties need to be far tougher with their own representatives, activists and supporters.

Thankfully, for the last few years I've been doing something every week which has managed to keep my pecker up. (Insert your own rude joke here.)

Chapter 13

THE PODCAST

Over the last few years, I started to feel like everything I cared about had been lost. The UK voted to leave the EU, the Labour Party fell into the hands of extremists, Donald Trump won the presidency, Britain is run by a populist and, although Scotland voted to remain in the UK, nationalists on both sides of the border are keen for that to end as soon as possible. It's all happened in the age of social media, where we talk to each other like dirt. It has been the worst political experience I've lived through. Event after event has felt like a catastrophe, like a motorway pile-up that never ends. Each tragedy is another juggernaut adding to the carnage. For years now I've felt politically homeless. Having spent so much of my life in the Labour Party, it felt strange to be outside of it. Not just outside of it but horrified by how nasty and irrelevant it had become. I didn't recognise it as the party I'd worked for. It had the same name and logo, but that's all that remained. It was as if someone had taken the engine out of a Mercedes. On the outside it might look like the same car as before, but when you lifted the bonnet you realised the engine had been replaced with a turnip. A very angry turnip.

Yet even in these dark times, there have been reasons to be positive. In 2013 I started a podcast called *The Political Party*. I wanted to put on a live event, which mixed topical comedy and a light-hearted interview with a big political name, that I could then broadcast to a wider audience. From my experience of working in politics and interviewing politicians on the radio, I knew how differently politicians behaved in private and when they were relaxed. It frustrated me that the public rarely got to see politicians the way I saw them, so I wanted to create a show that allowed them to be themselves. I was also frustrated by the way the media treated politicians. Combative interviews are a crucial part of a healthy democracy, but not every interview has to be like that. I couldn't see any other platform that was giving politicians an hour to be candid about their politics and their decisions. That doesn't mean I go easy on them; it just means the tone is informal and fair. I interview them in good faith and treat them like fellow human beings, rather than with suspicion or contempt. The result is that my guests drop their guard and tell me more than they do other interviewers. The only downside is that I am frequently told by audience members to stop booking Tories, because 'you're making me like them too much'.

I've always preferred talking to politicians I disagree with. I find them more interesting. I want to know what makes them a Conservative, a Brexiteer, a Scottish nationalist or a communist.

I like finding out how they reached a different conclusion to me and what politicised them. These conversations also make me question my own beliefs – and even if they only reinforce my opinions, they can help make my own thinking more nuanced. (Although I can't immediately recall when I've had my mind changed, so maybe I'm not as open-minded as I claim to be.) For many others, though, the pleasure of listening to someone you disagree with seems to have been lost. We follow accounts on Twitter that we agree with. We only read articles that we agree with. We quickly share things on social media, often without reading the content, because the headline seems to reinforce what we think. While an element of this is natural, completely ignoring any dissenting voices is unhealthy. Worse than that, it's boring. It is brain-fryingly tedious only hearing from people you agree with. I want to know what the other side thinks. This doesn't mean you have to follow individuals or organisations who are provocative or disrespectful, but it is healthy to open yourself up to the reasonable voices on all sides of the debate. Getting a good balance of political voices in your life is the same as trimming a rose bush. Avoid the pricks.

Before my show started on a monthly basis in February 2013, I had originally run a few ideas past my management. One idea was to create a satirical show, where I'd be the host and chat with different comedic correspondents playing different roles – a bit like the *Daily Show*, but live. I dismissed this idea, as simply the thought of all the admin involved with booking comedians and overseeing it stressed me. The other idea was more straightforward. I'd do a twenty-to-thirty-minute stand-up routine about the month in politics at the start of the show, have a drinks break and then interview a politician in front of the audience for an hour. I'm always wary of simple ideas, because I'm worried they demonstrate a lack of ambition or creative thinking, but in my experience the simpler ideas are the best. I could be ambitious with the writing or the way I approached the interview, so I didn't need to overthink the format. What was I going to do anyway? Bring on Charles Clarke to a full laser and lights show? Actually, that sounds amazing. I might try that next month.

I needed a venue fairly close to Parliament to make it easy for guests to get to after a day in the Commons or Lords. I figured Wednesday was the best night of the week to have it, as MPs go back to their constituencies on Thursday evenings and they also might be less likely to agree to something that could involve having a drink at the start of the week. My management team at Avalon were superb and found a beautiful venue that had just opened the year before. The St James Theatre on Palace Street is just off Victoria Street and around the corner from Buckingham Palace, so it was perfect. The plan was to do the show in its low-lit cabaret bar, where the dark-wood panelling lends it a conspiratorial feel and makes it feel like a back room in Parliament.

Once the venue, dates and guests were sorted, I just needed to find an audience. At this point I got that panic that all comedians get when they worry about sales. Stand-up comedy is a uniquely lonely and personal corner of the arts. In a play or in a band, you've at least got other people with you on stage, and even a solo singer can perform a great show to small numbers. Stand-up doesn't work in empty rooms. Trust me, I know. I wondered if I was making a massive mistake. Political stand-up and an interview with a politician might have been my idea of a great night, but would anyone else pay to watch it? When you think about it like that, it sounds like a terrible idea. It's not exactly *Les Mis*, is it? I couldn't imagine tourists in Leicester Square struggling to make up their mind between seeing *Phantom of the Opera* and Matt Forde interviewing Lembit Öpik. 'I know it's the most famous musical in the world, dear, but down the road there's some comedian we've never heard of interviewing a Lib Dem. We're only in London for one more night before we fly back to Kentucky. Let's make it count.'

Thankfully, people did turn up, mainly due to the phenomenal effort the publicity and live departments at Avalon put in to promote the show all across London. I put a lot of pressure on myself to make the show excellent. People have paid money for their tickets and some have booked a babysitter. I never want to put on a show that I haven't worked hard enough on, and I never want to go on stage hungover. I started a new routine when I began *The Political Party* that I still do seven years later and don't think I'll ever shake. In the month before each show, I look for stories every day that I can write material on. They all get saved in a big document and then, on the week of the show, I write every day from about 8 a.m. until 8 p.m. I don't touch a drop of alcohol in the days leading up to the gig, as I don't want to do anything that might compromise the quality of the show. This is probably overkill, but it's become part of the routine. Back in 2013, I used to imagine that if the show ever bedded in and ran for a sustained period of time, it would become easier to write and prepare for and that my nerves would recede. That has not happened. On the last Wednesday of every month I turn up at the venue, now renamed The Other Palace Theatre, and panic that what I've written is shit. I'll leave it up to you to listen back to a few and decide for yourself. I say that, but if it's really bad, it never makes it to the podcast, so you're already listening to the highlights. Which makes it even worse if you think it's shit. I'm now imagining you, a reader I don't know, going, 'Christ. And that was his best stuff.'

The interview excites me so much. I'll be thinking about it all month, making notes on my phone about things to ask them about. I can't wait. I am genuinely interested in what they have to say, so I'm never itching to butt in and interrupt. I only interject if I feel they're wandering off topic and losing the room, or if they're pushing their luck a bit and being cheeky. Before the interview starts, I'll have in mind a maximum of five things I want to ask them about. I'll hold these questions in mind, but I'll be more focussed on listening to their answers and following any leads that naturally present themselves. I want to make sure it's more like a conversation and I'm not just ticking questions off. I never take any notes on with me, which seems to help them relax. Part of the thrill is that talking is what politicians do, so the audience and I are getting to see them do politics live. There's really nowhere else where a political interview has been turned into a night out in London every month. I've interviewed a lot of footballers, but they don't bring a ball with them and score a goal during an interview. For the record, no politicians have done that either.

The audience deserve so much credit for making the show what it is. When it began, I used to start the interview by laying down the ground rules – that whoever the guest was, we'd be courteous to them and that heckling wasn't allowed. I didn't need to keep saying it. I probably didn't need to say it in the first place, but I didn't know much about my audience back then. They're a brilliant crowd. They come from every part of the political compass and from both sides of the Brexit divide, although they're probably a bit more Remainery than Leavey. They totally buy into the ethos of it and can laugh along with a guest they'd never vote for without feeling any pressure to agree with them. Many of the regulars don't share my politics, but they come every month regardless of who the guest is because they share my passion for engaging with individuals and ideas they disagree with. Being in a room with such a wonderful audience every month has helped me cope with all the negative aspects of politics in that time. They prove that most of us aren't unreasonable ideologues. They have their firmly held opinions, but they revel in sharing a room with people of differing political perspectives. It could be that or it could be that they just love getting smashed on red wine. Either way, I completely identify with them.

I can't hide my political beliefs, but I try to keep them out of the way during the interview. The guests and the audience know I'm a Blairite and it's usually referred to as a joke. I say it's a joke, but if I do go over the top and say that the 1997–2010 government were the best days any of us will ever have as long as we live, I'm only half joking. In a way, being around the centre ground makes it easier for me to host a show like *The Political Party*; my broadly pragmatic view of politics means I don't think it's heresy to talk to Tories. Although I still dress up as a chicken whenever I interview Lib Dems.

My Blairism has become a running theme, so when Tony Blair actually appeared on the show I did wonder if I'd left the show with nowhere else to go. For security reasons, I couldn't announce who the guest was. I got my mum, my sister, my girlfriend and a couple of pals in, but couldn't tell anyone who it was because if it got out – well, you can imagine. I mean, I like the guy, but I'm not taking a bullet for him.

The audience arrived not knowing what was about to unfold. I overheard someone say, 'If he hasn't announced it, it's bound to be some crap backbencher.' Cherie Blair was in the crowd and a couple of people had noticed, so a ripple ran around the room. Was Tony Blair going to turn up? Most people have never seen a prime minister or ex-prime minister in the flesh. Whatever you think of Tony Blair, he is one of the most influential figures in British history and someone who has continued to be globally influential after leaving office. Was he really going to appear at a cabaret bar on a Wednesday night? Yes, he was. When I announced him, the room exploded in a mixture of disbelief and excitement. I'll never forget the bloke on the second row who just mouthed to himself, 'What the fuck?'

I try and make every interview a mixture of light and shade – proper political discussion mixed with funny bits. We talked about Iraq, and it was important that I asked him difficult questions about it. In those moments, the power of the evening is laid bare – finally, the chance to see a former prime minister explaining his most unpopular decision to the general public. As well as being very serious, there were also some unexpectedly raucous moments. He revealed that he'd done stand-up comedy at university. As far as I knew, this was an exclusive and something I'd never heard before. I pushed him to remember what material he'd done and, after some resistance, he caved in and admitted he'd been part of a saucy *Star Trek* pastiche where he'd played a character called Captain Kink. I've never been able to get the image out of my mind. Good luck getting it out of yours.

The happiest and most surprising side effect of the podcast has been the friendships I've made with people I've really disagreed with. Pete Wishart from the SNP is someone I was terrified of. For years Pete was a ferocious opponent on social media, and I presumed from his online persona that he was the world's most unreasonable and angry man. We first met on *Question Time* when I had a massive row with Ken Livingstone, who'd made some typically daft remarks about 7/7. He obviously enjoyed the attention that spouting nonsense got him and went on to say even worse things a few years later. I entered the green room with trepidation, knowing that Pete was on the panel. It's not like I expected him to bite me or anything, but I was a bit nervous. He turned out to be the complete opposite of how I'd imagined: he was softly spoken and reasonable. I approached him in the way a rescue cat approaches a friendly human offering them food. I wanted to trust him, but I was wary that he was going to drug me and put me in a cage. He did neither and as a result we got on very well. Every Christmas Pete plays live music for the Christmas special of the podcast at the Bloomsbury Theatre with his parliamentary rock band of MPs, called MP4. Before he was an MP, Pete was a proper rock star and played keyboards in Runrig and Big Country. Runrig were big supporters of Scottish independence and played to huge crowds at Loch Lomond. They also played the Pyramid Stage at Glastonbury in 1992, making Jeremy Corbyn the second cantankerous MP to play it. I know Pete will read this, so, Pete, I'm joking. Put the cage down.

MP4 are a rock band of four MPs. As well as Pete Wishart (SNP, Perth and North Perthshire), the band consists of Greg Knight (Conservative, East Yorkshire) on drums, Ian Cawsey (Labour, Brigg and Goole) and Kevin Brennan (Labour, Cardiff West) on vocals and guitar. Ian sadly lost his seat at the 2010 election and the rest of the band joked that he'd have to leave and they'd become MP3. They're a brilliant live band and they make the Christmas specials a proper party. If you need a wedding band, book them. They've all been whips, so as well as great music, if you get them drunk, you'll get all sorts of political gossip out of them. Plus, if you pay them enough, they'll have to declare it, so you'll get your name in the MPs' Register of Interests. When you consider the political turbulence of the last few years, it's a miracle that a rock group of MPs containing a Brexiteer Tory, a Scottish nationalist and two Labour MPs – one of whom is WELSH – has managed to stay together. They're living proof that we can all get along. Bands are meant to be fractious anyway, but can you imagine what their green room is like? Blazing rows about whose turn it is to sort the drugs, made even worse by politics. 'Of course I had to pay for the cocaine. I end up paying for everything in this band. Just like Scotland has to pay for being part of your failing Union! Anyway, this song is called "Don't Look Back in Anger". A one, a two, a one, two, three, four . . .'

Another very memorable guest was Sayeeda Warsi, who paired up with Nick Clegg one Christmas and was exceptional. As well as being a brilliant political brain and a great thinker, Sayeeda is one of the funniest people I've ever met. This was back when Theresa May was prime minister. I asked Sayeeda for her assessment of her and she said, 'The prime minister's job goes against everything in her personality. It is the equivalent of me, a Muslim who eats halal, getting a job in a pig abattoir.' That line came out of nowhere and the audience loved it. It was tame compared to what was coming. As it was Christmas, I'd got some crackers for us to pull. Sayeeda won the cracker pull against Nick and against me. I casually asked her if she'd been practising and she responded that as a Muslim she was good with things that exploded. Holy shit. The place erupted in laughter. Nick Clegg had the look of a man who didn't know if he was allowed to laugh or not. In the space of half an hour Baroness Warsi had gone from Tory grandee to edgy comedian. I couldn't believe what I was witnessing: Sayeeda Warsi, Too Hot For TV.

The podcast has allowed me to chart the changing politics of the UK and build up a library of in-depth interviews with influential individuals that will be available forever. The pace of political change in the last few years is reflected in the back catalogue of episodes. When Luciana Berger, Chuka Umunna and others left the Labour Party to form a new political party, I was filled with hope. It was a bold and brave move and told the country that there were prominent Labour people who found Labour's antisemitism unacceptable and were prepared to do something about it. A few days later Conservative MPs Anna Soubry, Heidi Allen and Sarah Wollaston joined them in protest at the state of the Tory Party and out of a desire to form a new, moderate party. I was immensely excited and hastily arranged an event with four of them at short notice. It sold out in minutes. On the night, Heidi Allen, Ann Coffey, Mike Gapes and Chuka Umunna were exceptional. It wasn't so much their excitement about the future, it was the relief all of them felt now that they didn't have to be members of parties that had become poisonous. The burden of defending the indefensible, of suffering the company of bullies had become too great. Sadly, like an illegal rave, the party didn't last long. I think some raves have lasted longer. But I still admire them for taking a stand; the country needed to see that some MPs knew that both the Tories and Labour had drifted beyond acceptability.

Political talent deserves respect, wherever it exists. Just as football fans can appreciate a great goal scored by an opponent, in politics it's healthy to acknowledge the abilities of politicians on the other side. It's partly why the Corbyn years were so painful: there was an almost total lack of talent on Labour's front bench. It was like a social experiment where all the most useless people were put in charge of something to see what happens. You might as well have put a hamster in charge of a pet shop. I love Prime Minister's Questions, even though it's been terrible for years. It's not the most important test, but I love seeing a great parliamentary performance. I can watch BBC Parliament as a neutral, like a football scout would. Angus Robertson is an exceptional political talent, uniquely suited to the big stage. He only got two questions every week but managed to fit in five or six because of the way he worded them. He had something crucial to commanding the floor – composure. Angus is very good at the serious side of politics and has a lot of gravitas. He was one of my favourite guests because, as well as doing the serious stuff, he revealed a really silly sense of humour and spent the night impersonating football commentators, cockneys and Austrian psychologists. He didn't change my mind about independence, but he did give me an important reminder that although some politicians can appear serious or dour, some do that because they take politics seriously. They're still capable of being human beings. Who impersonate Austrian psychologists after a couple of whiskies.

The debates about the UK leaving the EU and Scotland leaving the UK trouble me more than party politics because they're so much bigger and they're such definite outcomes. Once they're decided, we won't get the chance to vote again in five years' time like we do with an election. That lack of consolation in the event of defeat makes me anxious. They feel like they're issues that are too big to be put at risk. It's why speaking to Brexiteers and independence supporters has been so important – it always slightly reduces my anxiety. I can't help myself believing that Brexiteers are on some level being deeply unreasonable. Maybe it's because so much of the argument to leave was clearly bullshit. See, I'm doing it again. I accept that there are different perspectives, but I worry about how casual the Leavers are about the consequences. This may be news to some Remainers, but a lot of the politicians who campaigned for Leave are great company. Brexit should not come between us as people. I really enjoyed interviewing the Chair of the European Research Group, Suella Braverman. She was funny, warm and modest. She really let her guard down and we laughed a lot. The ERG have taken on a mythical status since the EU referendum. I've been guilty in the past of insinuating that they're pretty much a cult who commit human sacrifice. I mean, I don't know for sure that they definitely don't but after interviewing Suella I'm at least less inclined to believe it.

The one guest who has really eluded me so far is Jeremy Corbyn, which may sound obvious – I've not exactly ingratiated myself to him. But I've had Corbyn loyalists like Jon Lansman and Rebecca Long-Bailey on the show and he'd get exactly the same treatment I give every guest. If anything, I'd probably be even nicer to him for fear of looking biased the other way. I'm fascinated by Corbyn; he had an unfortunate tendency to be tetchy in media interviews, so I want to see what he's like when he's relaxed over a longer interview. I'd be totally fair with him, as I am with everyone, because that's the point of the night. I can't break the rules for any guest and anyway, I want to have a genuine chat with him. I can't imagine his staff would talk him into doing it. 'Jeremy, you've got to do Matt Forde's podcast, he talks about Tony Blair almost as much as you do!' On the off chance that he's reading this, then, Jeremy, call me. Let's make it happen. I realise I'm making it sound like Joshua v Fury in Vegas but, like that, it's the match-up that the public want to see. That a very small number of the public want to see.

I could easily keep recounting some of the highlights of the show and I'm worried I've done that too much already, like some name-dropping dinner party bore with red wine stains round his mouth. So many of the guests have been excellent: Ruth Davidson, Jess Phillips, David Lammy, Ken Clarke, Alastair Campbell, Ed Balls, Rosena Allin-Khan, Keir Starmer, Emily Thornberry, William Hague, George Osborne, Johnny Mercer, James Cleverly and so many more. I could fill a library of books with anecdotes about them. I'm sure it's the same for listeners of the show, but I learn something from each of them, even if it's just a new perspective on an issue. If there's one common theme that runs through the show, it's the importance of and challenges of leadership. Whether it's talking to former party leaders like Paddy Ashdown, Jo Swinson or Neil Kinnock, or leaders currently in charge of big cities like Sadiq Khan or countries like Nicola Sturgeon, or former cabinet members like Michael Heseltine, Alistair Darling or Justine Greening, the insights on leadership are the most fascinating. That probably sounds obvious, but I don't think enough of us think about leadership and the realities of it. Don't worry, I'm not about to launch into tedious management speak, but if you could imaginise a thinkspace, we can delivery-fixate a solution-stratagem axis, yeah? Guys?

I've never led a political party or country and, thankfully for all of us, I never will. I'd end up leveraging the total assets of the British state to get Nottingham Forest into the Premier League. Actually, the idea is growing on me. This isn't an exhaustive list in any particular order but the things I hear more regularly about leadership from leaders and those close to them are:

- Always put the country before the party. You owe your position in part to the party, but you have to remember who your audience is when you're a national leader. The public feel a sense of ownership over you. Party members don't always represent mainstream public opinion.
- Choose a leader who is impressive. It is impossible if they're not. This is more a lesson for members, affiliates and colleagues. It doesn't matter how much you believe in the ideas, if the leader is dim or dull, you're handing victory to your opponents. Leading a country is the ultimate important job. People expect that individual to be impressive.

- Strike early. Do big, bold or more difficult things early on in your leadership. You set a tone of action and you've got the goodwill to spend. Challengers are less likely to come for you immediately after a victory.
- Don't pretend to be perfect. You can't do everything, so prioritise and explain your priorities. Accept that you'll make mistakes. It's about outcomes, so if a policy isn't working, adjust or scrap it.
- Every leader wishes they'd been bolder. Every leader I've spoken to wishes they'd trusted their instincts more. In some cases that wouldn't have been the right thing to do, but it does mean that if you're ultimately accountable for what happens, make sure you believe in what you're doing. If you feel blown along by other people, that regret will eat away at you once you cease to be leader.

Well, that's pretty much it. You're ready to be prime minister now. If you do make it there, stick me in the Lords or something as thanks.

CONCLUSIONS

My relationship with politics has changed. I entered it as an activist, worked in it as a professional and now take the piss out of it for a living. I'm still an obsessive. I still pore over every story, devour political biographies, talk to politicians of all parties regularly and curse the decisions of our leaders. I care about it. No matter how bad things get, I'll never believe that all politicians are the same, that they're all in it for themselves or that they're all corrupt. Experience and evidence prove this to be untrue. There are gifted, caring and talented politicians everywhere and they deserve our support instead of being lumped in with all the cretins.

I'll always love reading polling, policy documents and select committee reports. I'll go to party conferences again and I'll still go to Parliament on a day off, sit in the public gallery and watch a debate on a subject I know nothing about. If you've never done it, promise me you'll go. Just nip in on a quiet afternoon and watch it for an hour or so. You'll see politics being done respectfully and thoughtfully with MPs from different parties and places reasoning with each other maturely. Unless you've got tickets for PMQs, in which case you'll see grown adults behaving like chimps. Which is way better.

The last few years have been bruising for so many of us. It's not that we can't handle dissent, it's that we can't handle it done in this way. Political disagreement is welcome, but not when it's accompanied by racism or a desire to completely trash the character of our opponents. Most of us can disagree without resorting to insults or hurtful language. Mainstream politics has to follow suit. Parties and movements should no longer tolerate their nastier elements and should boot them out, if only for their own self-interest. Hordes of online bullies have held back the progress of the Labour Party, the Conservative Party and the Scottish independence movement. If leaders are embarrassed by the more extreme elements of their parties, they should take action against them. Not just to protect decent people from abuse, but to prevent the problem from growing. In Labour's case, the bullies were able to seize control of the party. If it happens again, the results will be the same. Good people will be hounded out and the party will continue to lose elections. It's a sign of how warped politics has become that some people would see that as a positive result.

I still feel politically homeless, despite Keir Starmer becoming Labour leader. To say he's a massive improvement on Jeremy Corbyn doesn't adequately reflect the scale of the change. It's like replacing a dead mouse with, well, Keir Starmer. His leadership on tackling antisemitism has been excellent so far. He seems prime ministerial and it's the first time in a decade that Labour has a better candidate for the office of prime minister than the Tories. His election as leader is an important correction for our democracy. Starmer highlights what an indulgent choice Boris Johnson was. He's everything that Johnson isn't. He's serious, reasonable and appears to act in the national interest. But it's not Starmer I worry about, it's the Labour Party. Current polling suggests that the country feels the same way – Starmer is much more popular than Johnson, but Labour are still behind the Tories in the polls. The party is still in a mess. Despite a lot of Corbyn's fans leaving, it's still a party too far to the left and a party unable to be honest with itself about what the country wants. To win, I think Starmer has to make a big deal about moving on from the Corbyn years, and that means doing more than acting on anti-semitism. It means saying to the country, 'For at least the last five years we have insulted you by ignoring you. I am embarrassed by it and I will not let that happen again. This party is no longer the party of Jeremy Corbyn and Momentum. Those ideas are no longer welcome. We are a national party; we love our country and we will no longer seek to divide people but unite them. I know it will take time to win back your trust but we are facing a crisis because we have the worst government in living memory and we all need to come together to make our country better.' Perhaps it's wishful thinking, but as I'm fantasising, wouldn't it be great if he could add at the end, 'Oh, and if I'm prime minister, you'll get a free Greggs pasty every day that I'm in charge.' Just to fully seal the (meal) deal.

We're leaving the European Union and that has dire geo-political implications. It emboldens Putin and China and it harms our economy. I'd love to think that we'll decide to rejoin the EU one day, but that day is probably a long way off. Those of us who want to see it need to learn from our opponents. For forty years they were relentless in attacking our place in Europe. We need to regularly make the positive case for European membership, ready for the time should it come. Which makes it sound like the rapture, but you know what I mean. The same goes for saving the UK. We know the break-up of the UK is what our enemies want. They want a powerful Western democracy to split and turn in on itself. We need to make the patriotic Scottish case for staying in the Union. In fact, we need to make the case for the Union in England, too, and not be complacent that people in England take it for granted. We should have the debates we should have been having these last few years, about how we use automation and new technologies to improve our environment as well as our healthcare, education and economy. I've no doubt those debates will still end up in some sort of culture war, with campaigns for British jobs for British robots.

The centre ground needs to rediscover its passion. If preventing populism and nationalism aren't good enough incentives to defend democracy and decency, then there's no hope. Railing against Brexit raised the game of a generation of politicians who'd only known Parliament in relatively stable times. We saw how it made talented politicians like Chuka Umunna and Anna Soubry far more compelling communicators. The upheaval created by the coronavirus will sharpen the acumen of a whole new cohort. People who never thought they'd want to go into politics will be inspired to, through a desire to tidy up the mess and improve things. The pandemic has the potential to start the biggest national conversation we've ever had about how our country should work. It has highlighted the strengths and weaknesses of our system and after a bruising collective experience – especially one with a high death toll – the public are more alert to the dangers of under-resourcing places like care homes. The optimist in me hopes that this will lead to a new era of tackling deep systemic inequality and creating a more equal and successful country. The pessimist in me thinks we'll waste our time arguing with pillocks who enjoy rebelling against the wearing of face masks during a lethal pandemic.

We must always be vigilant and take political sores seriously. If we ignore them and don't treat them, they fester and become worse and we end up doing something like leaving the European Union. Politicians who put problems off are only acting out of self-preservation. We need to reward politicians who deliver hard truths and not those who pander to us. They're only in it to hold office and don't want to take any difficult decisions. That means nothing changes, so there's no point in them. We also need to reward politicians who unite and not those who divide. Blaming other people for our problems is the oldest trick in politics and we need to stop falling for it. They'll wrap it up as something else and they'll rebrand it, but you can always spot it. They'll say it's just for now, that things have changed or, the new favourite, that we actually deepen our relationship with our neighbours by severing all ties. Ah yes, just as you demonstrate your true love for someone by divorcing them.

You're not always going to get what you want. In politics it's easy to feel that you don't get what you want any of the time. This is almost certainly untrue. There'll always be something to take heart from. Even if you think most of what the government did during the coronavirus crisis was a calamity, you probably agreed with the furlough scheme. Even if you disagreed with that, you might be reassured by the role opposition politicians have played in holding the government to account. Winning is crucial for political parties, but for the rest of us who have to live with outcomes we didn't vote for, we can feel taunted by the defeat. That's why it's important to seek out opponents who you like. Listen to their perspective on why something you don't like is something that they really value. If there's one thing you take away from this book, let it be that engaging with people you disagree with can be deeply satisfying. You don't just have to endure it, you can really enjoy it. You'll almost always find that you hadn't considered an aspect of the debate or hadn't appreciated that someone who'd led their life instead of yours would reach that conclusion. They may be your opponents in politics, but they don't have to be your opponents in life. There'll be so much you have in common, so find it.

That brings us to the end. I can't thank you enough for reading this book. Most people don't ever get the chance to write a book, especially if they're from backgrounds like mine. I hope I've done justice to the opportunity I've been given. Whatever your politics, I hope you've taken my points with the goodwill in which they're intended, and I hope you've found it useful in some way. Even if it's just to rest your laptop on. Have a lovely day and I'll see you on the road sometime.

And that is that.

The End.

ACKNOWLEDGEMENTS

In comedy it's quite rare to be given a public platform to thank the people who've helped you. You say thanks in private at the end of projects – TV series, tours, radio shows – but I've never had the chance before to put my thanks on the record to some brilliant people who've helped my career.

Jon Thoday at Avalon is an exceptional agent. His wisdom and guidance have been invaluable since he signed me ten years ago. There's no way I'd have got this far without him. He's so persuasive he even convinced me, a committed republican, to perform at the Royal Variety Show and shake hands with Prince Harry.

Katy Follain at Quercus edited the book and helped me at every stage. At the start of the process I asked her to give me brutal feedback. She did and the result is that this book is a far better read than if Katy had not been involved. Alison Mac-Donald was also a huge help, improving the quality of the book with excellent advice. It's been a delight publishing this book with Quercus, who've given me the encouragement I needed throughout.

Katie McKay at Avalon made the book happen. She pushed me

to come up with the idea and got it commissioned. I'll always be grateful to her for this wonderful opportunity.

Jules Lom, Julien Matthews, Victoria Wedderburn, Qasim Salam, Sophia Surjadi, Mary-Grace Brunker, Seth Lavell, Alice Seyfang, Steff Easom and everyone at Avalon have been hugely supportive over many years. Getting me work, organising my diary, booking and promoting tours and Edinburgh runs, but mainly reassuring me that I'm not going to die on my arse and that I've not put on too much weight.

Daisy Knight and Richard Garvin help make *The Political Party* podcast the success that it is. They're both talented producers who contribute much more than just work. They are a constant source of great ideas and sound advice, but they mainly reassure me that I'm not going to die on my arse and that I've not put on too much weight.

My wonderful girlfriend, Laura, deserves a lot of thanks for this book being what it is, mainly because she let me use the spare room to write it, which meant she had to work on the settee for months. She is endlessly supportive of me pursuing a line of work that mainly involves me putting on silly voices, including various Scottish ones she is clearly growing tired of.

Finally, my career wouldn't exist without public support. To everyone who's ever come to see me perform live, downloaded the podcast, said something positive to or about me on social media, and to everyone who bought this book, thank you. It means the world, cheers.